The Spirit of Peace

Pentecost and Affliction in the Middle East

— MARY C. GREY —

Sacristy Press

Sacristy Press
PO Box 612, Durham, DH1 9HT

www.sacristy.co.uk

First published in 2015 by Sacristy Press, Durham

Sacristy Limited, registered in England & Wales, number 7565667

British Library Cataloguing-in-Publication Data
A catalogue record for the book is available from the British Library

ISBN 978-1-908381-20-0

Dedicated to my dear sister Margaret who died as this book reached completion

Preface

How to write a Preface for a situation that is ever evolving? For a conflict seemingly without a peaceful resolution, at least in the near future? But, in a sense, this gave a significant rationale for this book. Nearing the end of the third book of the trilogy,[1] I was almost overwhelmed by the tragedy of the continuing conflict in so many Middle Eastern countries. This was accompanied by my own personal sorrow over the sudden death of a younger sister.

If I had not thought or felt so strongly about these conflicts before I began, I certainly do so now; the question that arises from the depths is where is the Holy Spirit in this situation of affliction of Christians in Middle Eastern countries? This makes this book far more than a coherent ending to a trilogy that began with Advent, continuing with Easter, and now concluding with Pentecost: it is a humble response to the key existential cry rising up from the people of lands where Christianity is rooted, and where it grew from the inspiration of the earliest disciples of Christ.

That cry comes too from many groups to which I owe gratitude and inspiration: to Sabeel in Jerusalem, especially to Cedar Duaybis and Samia Khoury; to the Arab Education Institute in Bethlehem, especially to Dr Toine van Teeffelen; to Zoughbi Zoughbi and his family of Wi'am, Bethlehem; and also to the many groups in the UK who act in solidarity, especially to Mariam Tadros of Embrace the Middle East and to her family; and to my colleagues in Living Stones of the Holy Land.

In the context of also preparing for the funeral of our sister, I want to mention especially my brothers and sisters with gratitude for the values and memories we share. It is also the year when Nicholas and I give thanks for 50 years since our wedding. Without the commitment to justice we have shared for half a century, this book would not have been written.

Mary Grey
May 2014

Notes

1. Mary Grey, *The Advent of Peace: A Gospel Journey to Christmas* (London: SPCK, 2010); and *idem*, *The Resurrection of Peace: A Gospel Journey to Easter and Beyond* (London: SPCK, 2012).

Contents

INTRODUCTION

Whatever happened to the Arab Spring? The threatened situation of Christians in the Middle East.

When I began my previous book, *The Resurrection of Peace,* in 2011 an unexpected sense of optimism was in the air. Despite being conscious of the ongoing suffering in Israel and Palestine, I wrote that a new mood had emerged in the Middle East in December 2010:

> Called the Arab Spring, this movement began in Tunisia, followed by uprisings in Egypt, Libya, Syria, Yemen and Bahrain. Each conflict has its own unique character, and it is by no means clear, over one year later, when the Arab Spring has moved into autumn, winter and another spring is near, whether the outcomes will be positive for freedom for suffering communities in every case. Syria is currently undergoing unspeakable suffering. Every day brings new tensions—but also hope.[1]

Church leaders from all denominations expressed their hopes as to the outcomes. There was an overwhelming feeling across the entire region that ordinary people wanted to be heard, that people—both Muslims and Christians—longed for a democratic, open society.

But now, over three years later, there is a completely different mood. In Tahrir Square, Cairo, where the peaceful revolution of the Arab Spring in Egypt is said to have begun, there are still regular gatherings and protests.

I was in Tahrir Square on 1 May (traditional Labour Day) in 2013, where the Egyptian people, totally disillusioned with events after the uprising, were demonstrating for just wages; their mood, although peaceful, was far from euphoric. Events would worsen as the months went on. In Syria, the civil war has worsened catastrophically, causing a humanitarian crisis of frightening proportions in regard to the refugees now living in camps in Jordan, Turkey, and Lebanon, as well as in Syria itself. The United Nations has declared that the enormity of this crisis is unique.

Due to these conflicts, but not exclusively so, there is an exodus of enormous proportions of Syrian Christians and Muslims to Europe, Australia, the United States, and other parts of the world, as there has been for some time of Coptic Christians from Egypt and Christians from most Middle Eastern countries. The Chaldean Christian Church in Iraq has been decimated.[2] Meanwhile, on the ground in Israel and Palestine, the suffering created by the Israeli Occupation of the West Bank continues and worsens, as does the misery of the people of Gaza. From Palestine also the flight of Christians continues: last year (2013) I heard the Lutheran bishop in Jerusalem, Mounir Younan, pleading for his flock to have the courage to stay in the Holy Land and struggle on for a peaceful end to the conflict.

Almost echoing my sense of despair, an interview by Andrea Tornelli with the (now retired) Archbishop of Galilee, Elias Chacour (*Vatican Insider*, 7 June, 2013), presents the Archbishop as declaring that the so-called Arab Spring has not delivered on its promise.[3] The Archbishop, in Haifa (Israel), said:

> Arab Spring is not the right term. This was no spring. It was a monumental bloodbath. So many died, but the biggest losers are the Christians . . .

Elias Chacour until 2014, presided over one of the largest communities of Arab Catholics in Israel as Archbishop of the Melkite Greek Catholic Church in Akko, Haifa, Nazareth, and All Galilee (the Melkite Church is in communion with Rome).The Church has eighty thousand faithful, thirty-two parishes and twenty-eight priests. The Archbishop—who has been inspirational to international audiences through his books, lectures, his own life-history,[4] and his willingness to welcome guests—met with *Vatican Insider* and other Italian media at his residence in the Israeli city of Haifa; his own projects are shining examples of peaceful coexistence between religions in the Holy Land, something he has striven for all his life. During this meeting—along with other topics—he expressed his concerns about the fate of Christians who have been forced to flee Syria. He said (emphasis is mine):

> I do not know why so many lost their lives in the Arab "Spring"—which *was not a spring at all since it produced no fruits and new life was nowhere to be seen.* The Chaldean bishop in the U.S., Ibrahim Ibrahim told me that Detroit's 4,000 Chaldean Christians have now become 130 thousand because many fled the countries where they had previously been living. I ask myself why the West is doing nothing to stop what is going on in Syria. 160 little Christian villages have been completely abandoned. Many are fleeing to Lebanon but we do not know how many. I saw our bishop of Damascus cry like a baby: every single Christian in Syria needs our help; they need every bit of bread and every glass of water they can get . . .[5]

Strong words here! And things have deteriorated seriously since he made this speech. Archbishop Chacour also said all that has happened in Tunisia, Egypt, Libya, and Syria over the past few years has been "a turning point in Islamic history":

> Before, leaders would engage in power struggle without involving the public. We were not happy with the totalitarian regimes but we are not happy today either. This is partly because of the risk of Islamic sharia law coming into force, which would be abominable. We don't know what will happen further on down the line.[6]

Nor can the West shun responsibility for the chaos resulting in some countries after our intervention. In Libya, for example, where the West cooperated in the overthrow of Colonel Gadaffi, many human rights abuses followed; abuses which were ignored by the West. Owen Jones, in an article entitled "Libya is a disaster we helped create: we cannot stay silent" writes:

> There is a real prospect of the country collapsing into civil war or even breaking up. Unless there are negotiated settlements to its multiple problems, Libya will surely continue its descent into mayhem, and the region could be dragged into the mire with it.[7]

But to give way to despair is to be unfaithful to the Scriptural message of joy and hope in the Resurrection. None of the Christian Churches in the Middle East are doing this: on the contrary, they are a beacon of shining light in the darkness, contrasting with the (sometimes) weaker faith of Christians in the secular West who do not face persecution on a regular basis.

Why "The Spirit of Peace"?

In *The Advent of Peace* I explored the Gospel story of Advent and Christmas:[8] I journeyed with Mary and Joseph to Bethlehem, both in the context of the Gospel story as well as in the contemporary realities in which the people of Bethlehem struggle amidst the daily humiliations of the Israeli Occupation. In the second book, *The Resurrection of Peace*,[9] the focus was principally on Galilee: I explored the ministry of Jesus at the lake-side villages by the Sea of Challenge with a special focus on his non-violent stance in the context of the Roman occupation. It was this stance for which he paid the ultimate price of a violent death, which offers inspiration for the Christian Palestinian people today in the continuing conflict that has now lasted for over sixty years.

At the end of the book, I left the fledgling post-resurrection Christian community, newly energised, on the open road to Galilee, with their mission to proclaim the Gospel to the ends of the earth.

But how could it actually be left there? There is still another story to be told. As we learn in *Acts of the Apostles* as well as in *The Letters of St Paul*, what follows is the dramatic story of the Holy Spirit who empowered the apostles at Pentecost and reminded them that the Gospel imperative was to be proclaimed and spread to the ends of the earth. So what has changed for the countries of the Middle East since these times? Like the young Church communities which endured persecution after the death of Jesus, they are now seeking the courage to endure in ever-new threats to their very existence. It is the power of the Spirit, both then and now, that inspires and underpins this endurance. At the same time, new dimensions of the Spirit's power unfold for new and ever-changing circumstances.

And this is not an unengaged exploration: Paul, after a visionary experience, answered the call of the Macedonians: "Come over here and help us" (Acts 16.6–7).[10] In our own times, will we Christians in the West and all people of good heed the appeals of Archbishop Elias Chacour of Galilee and the many Church leaders of Middle Eastern countries for help? But not only the appeal of Church leaders: countless numbers of ordinary people have the greatest claim on our hearts: "Come over here and help us before it is too late!"

So, I embark on another journey. Following the energies of the Spirit who inspires the search for truth and justice throughout the ages, I follow the struggles of some of the early Christian communities: both the disciples who sowed the seeds and those who were focused on the growth of community. At the same time, I examine the work of the Spirit today in some of the afflicted countries—Gaza, Syria, Egypt, and the Holy Land—where the Christian story began and continues to unfold.[11]

Using both sacred texts and contemporary accounts, this will be an exploration of the many dimensions and facets of the Holy Spirit as leading into the Unknown, as Depth, as searching for Truth, Beauty and Illumination, as Justice, Bridge-building, Hope, and other such dimensions. The movement of the Spirit is experienced in the Holy Lands as urgent and dynamic, but because this is a journey among people who experience persecution then and now, I begin with asking what it means to do theology experienced as *affliction.*

Notes

1. Grey, *The Resurrection of Peace*, p. 1.
2. See Suha Rassam, *Christanity in Iraq* (Leominster: Gracewing, 2005, reprinted 2010).
3. Andrea Tornelli interview with Archbishop (ret.) Elias Chacour, *Vatican Inside* (7 June 2013), <http://vaticaninsider.lastampa.it/en/world-news/detail/articolo/medio-oriente-middle-east-medio-oriente-25187/>.
4. See Elias Chacour and Mary Jensen, *We belong to the Land* (Indiana: University of Notre Dame Press, 2001); and Elias Chacour and David Hazard, *Blood Brothers* (New Jersey: Chosen Books, 1984).
5. Tornelli interview with Chacour
6. *Ibid.*
7. Owen Jones, "Libya is a disaster we helped create: we cannot stay silent", in *The Guardian* (24 March 2014), <http://www.theguardian.com/commentisfree/2014/mar/24/libya-disaster-shames-western-interventionists>.
8. Grey, *The Advent of Peace*.
9. Grey, *The Resurrection of Peace*.
10. See the discussion in Chapter 6.
11. I hope the reader will be patient with the fact that inevitably this is an unfolding story: when this book appears, events will have developed beyond what I am able to say at the time of writing.

CHAPTER 1

Doing theology in Ayacucho: forsakenness and affliction as themes for Christian theology in the Middle East

> As I worked in the factory, indistinguishable to all eyes, including my own, the affliction of others entered into my flesh and my soul . . .
>
> In the realm of suffering, affliction is something apart, specific and irreducible . . . It takes possession of the soul and marks it through and through with its own particular mark, the mark of slavery.
>
> ***Simone Weil***[1]

What has *affliction* as a theme to do with Ayacucho? How can Ayacucho have any connection with the Middle East? Ayacucho is a mountain village of great poverty and violence in Peru. The village was renamed Ayacucho by Simón Bolívar after the battle of 1825; a Venezuelan political revolutionary, he led several South American countries to freedom from Spanish colonialism. Today, Ayacucho has become a symbol both of suffering and hope. This is especially because the Peruvian theologian, Fr Gustavo Gutiérrez, often called "the Father of Liberation Theology", wrote an inspirational article some years ago, "How can God be discussed from the perspective of Ayacucho?",[2] in which he saw the poverty and suffering of the people of this village as paradigm for his life's work in Liberation Theology.

Gutiérrez raised this challenge because Liberation Theology does not start from the abstract categories of traditional systematic theology, but begins, rather, with actual life situations of suffering and oppression, asking penetrating questions about the structural causes of these. The conviction that God is on the side of the poor is the lifeblood of this theology. Gustavo Gutiérrez faces with courage the challenge of the very possibility of talking about God in such a desperate situation:

> Is it possible to talk about a God who wants justice in a situation of poverty and oppression? How can the God of life be proclaimed to people who are suffering premature and unjust death? . . . What language can be found to tell those who are not seen as integral persons that they are sons and daughters of God?[3]

How to talk about Christ, too, is part of the challenge. Does believing that Jesus Christ is Liberator, breaking the chains of oppression, really empower the struggle of ordinary people for justice? Liberation Christology proclaims that Jesus not only suffers in solidarity with the desperate situation of impoverished people but is a powerful source of hope that freedom and flourishing will be experienced in their own lifetimes.[4]

The ideas explored in this book are inspired by questions raised in "How can God be discussed from the perspective of Ayacucho?", and I face Gutiérrez's challenge from the context of Middle Eastern Christianity, now struggling for its very survival.

Readers may, of course, respond that a better example and a city more universally well-known for poverty and suffering might be, for example, Calcutta (Kolkata) in India, or Sarajevo at the height of the Balkans War. Sadly, examples of poverty-stricken cities abound in every continent and have always done so through the ages. What has changed is that this context has now become a new jumping off point for Christian theology. This is not to say that there have not been many great people concerned about poverty and injustice in the history of Christianity. On the contrary, the simplicity and concern for poor people of saints like Francis of Assisi are the bright stars of our past. Yet the life work and commitment of Gutiérrez has blazed a trail for many theologians from different continents who place the call to justice and liberation at the heart of their theology. And this has become a promising new start for a theology embodying the very integrity of commitment to working for justice. This new starting point has been encouraged by the election of Pope Francis in 2013 who has declared that he wants the church to be a Church of the poor and for the poor. This aim continues to be an inspiration even beyond the boundaries of the Christian Church.

Engaged theologians like Gutiérrez see theology as a "second level" act. The first act is *praxis,* or committed, active theology, meaning a concrete solidarity with suffering communities and a struggle for justice with them. Theology then reflects and inspires the next level of *praxis,* or reflection on this struggle and engagement, giving rise to new action. But a deeper look at the context of the struggle and suffering is required. For that I first turn to Simone Weil—cited at the beginning of this chapter.

Affliction as starting point for the Middle-Eastern context

Figure 1: Simone Weil[5]

Simone Weil was a sensitive, brilliant French philosopher and mystic of Jewish background, who lived through the events of the Second World War in solidarity with the French working class in occupied France. She struggled to be in solidarity with working people by labouring long hours in a factory, which almost ruined her health. Leaving France for America, she was immediately called back to serve the French provisional government in Britain and sailed for London. Yet she still insisted on sharing the hardships of those she had left behind in France, refusing the extra nourishment prescribed by her doctors. Her health soon worsened and she was admitted to the Middlesex Hospital in April, 1943, later being transferred to a sanatorium in Ashford, where she died of tuberculosis a few months later.[6] Although she was a person of deep faith and prayer, she never formally became a Christian, feeling strongly that her vocation was to one of "waiting" and witnessing from this stance.

Her relevance for this exploration is not so much her own spiritual journey, for which her writings are still considered spiritual classics. It is specifically her reflections on affliction, situated as they are in a context of German-occupied France and in her first-hand experience of the annihilating effects of poverty on the entire human spirit.

The comparison with Israel/Palestine/Gaza is obvious at a superficial level, given that the Occupation of the West Bank has lasted over forty-seven years. The resulting poverty and worsening humiliation of the Palestinians has been well-described by many writers in detail, by Palestinians themselves, by Israeli commentators like Gideon Levy, and by Western analysts.[7] But all too often this sounds like a never-ending catalogue of woes, and we are unable to take in and to respond to the complexity of issues involved. Can we reach a better understanding of what Palestinian people endure on a daily basis by reflecting on what Simone Weil writes about affliction?

What Weil—writing from her own context—reveals, is the woundedness of affliction which is at a far deeper level than that of mere physical suffering (emphasis is mine):

> The great enigma of human life is not suffering but affliction. It is not surprising that the innocent are killed, tortured, driven from their country, made destitute or reduced

> to slavery, imprisoned in camps or cells, since there are criminals to perform such actions. It is not surprising that disease is the cause of long sufferings, which paralyse life and make it into an image of death . . . *But it is surprising that God should have given affliction the power to seize the very souls of the innocent and to take possession of them as their sovereign lord.*[8]

Affliction, she writes, gives the experience of abandonment and forsakenness. It hardens and discourages us:

> . . . Because, like a red-hot iron it stamps the soul to its very depths with the disgust and even the very self-hatred and sense of guilt and defilement which crime logically should produce but actually does not.[9]

Affliction makes God appear absent for a while, "more absent than a dead man, more absent than light in the utter darkness of a cell".[10] Affliction made the crucified Jesus cry out: "My God, my God, why hast thou forsaken me?" (Mark 15.33–34). But, ultimately, he died with a cry of faith on his lips. The Biblical figure of Job, Weil believes, was an afflicted man. Affliction makes him cry out against God and curse the day of his birth (Job 3.11, 20–23).

Gutiérrez—in another work—also invokes Job not only as an afflicted man, but as a just man, for whom concern for justice was the supreme value of his life.[11] Indeed, Job gives one of the most radical analyses and insights contained in the Scriptures as to the oppression of the poor by the powerful:

> The wicked move boundary marks away,
> They carry off flock and shepherd.
> They drive away the orphan's donkey,
> As security they seize the widow's ox.
> The needy have to keep out of the way,
> Poor country people have to keep out of sight.
> Like wild desert donkeys, they go out to work,

> Searching from dawn for food,
> And at evening for something on
> which to feed their children.[12]

Finally, as the Book of Job tells us, Job is vindicated. He has not discovered the meaning of suffering—nor did Simone Weil—but he is rewarded for his faithfulness and steadfastness, and is brought to a new understanding of the freedom of God's love.[13]

The second connection with the situation of the Palestinians is that *affliction* describes their situation of humiliation, poverty, and violence. Again, I wrestle with Gutiérrez's question: how to speak about God in this context, how is God present except as absence? This liberation theologian, with a lifetime of commitment to seeking justice for some of the poorest and most abandoned people, writes:

> Some years ago, J. B. Metz, with great human and Christian sensitivity, asked how God could possibly be discussed after the horrendous experience of Auschwitz. Centuries ago, Bartolomé de los Casas stated that he had seen Christ scourged a thousand times in the Indians of Latin America; in the same context, I ask how God can be discussed not after but *during* Ayacucho! The question undoubtedly implies more than our capacity to reply.[14]

How to speak about God *now*, during this situation of escalating misery, encapsulates the very poignancy of this book's search. But there is an added dimension: this is that it is frequently the horrendous scale of suffering of the Jewish people in Auschwitz and many other death camps in the Second World War, as a result of Hitler's policies, that causes a certain blindness and denial as to the present suffering of the Palestinians for which the Israeli government is largely responsible.[15]

Affliction evokes not only the daily suffering of the people of the West Bank and Gaza, and the forgotten Palestinians in Israel,[16] the stalemate as to peace talks, and denial of the right of return of the refugees to their homes (a right enshrined in United Nations Resolution 194),[17] but also the denial of the truth of what actually happened in the *Nakba*, "catastrophe", the driving out of 800,000 Palestinian from their homes in 1948 and the loss of 533 villages.[18] Israel continues to date the Occupation from 1967.

According to Israeli historian Ilan Pappé, two manifestations of this denial have to be confronted. The first was the fact that international peace-brokers side-lined the Palestinian cause and concerns from any future arrangement or agreement. The second was:

> The categorical refusal of the Israelis to acknowledge the *Nakba* and their absolute unwillingness to be held accountable, legally and morally, for the ethnic cleansing they committed in 1948.[19]

Israel's insistence that nothing prior to 1967 will be included in any negotiations totally removes the right of return of the Palestinian refugees from any peace negotiations. We are drawing close to the heart of what *affliction* means in this context. The Israelis seem unable to acknowledge the trauma they inflicted on the Palestinians in 1948, and this is in stark contrast with the Palestinian narrative which they live to this day as ongoing affliction. The denial of memory—or *memoricide,* as Pappé calls it[20]—is an insidious form of persecution. Yet it is impossible to kill a people's memory. As Philippe Gaillard, head of the Red Cross delegation in Kigali, wrote in the context of the Rwandan genocide (1994):

> You may kill as many people as you want, but you cannot kill their memory. Memory is the most invisible and resistant material you can find on earth. You cannot cut it like a diamond, you cannot shoot at it, because you cannot see it; nevertheless it is everywhere, all around you, in the silence, unspoken suffering, whispers and absent looks.[21]

All the attempts to remove evidence of the ancient Palestinian villages, to rename them,[22] to forest the area in order to conceal them, and to forbid any reference to *Al Nakba* in Israeli school textbooks have failed to eradicate its memory. Murals of their old villages are painted on the walls of refugee camps, as I have witnessed in Bethlehem. Survivors of *Al Nakba* still sleep with the key of the front door under their pillows in hope of returning home. Nakba Day is commemorated each year on 15 May. But to have the truth of the past denied public acknowledgment is affliction indeed. It is not unlike what—from a completely different context—Korean Minjung theology describes as *han*. Minjung theology developed in the 1970s out of the suffering and oppression of South Korean Christians. *Han* is described as the feeling of deeply internalized lamentations and anger. It can be accumulated, transmitted, and inherited, boiling in the blood of the Minjung people. But in the case of the Palestinians, affliction is endured or sustained not only with anger, but with a growing Christian spirituality inspired by the concept of *sumud*.

Palestinian *sumud*—a source of strength for an afflicted people.

Sumud is an Arabic word meaning "steadfastness", "perseverance", and "resilience". Originating in a political context in the 1970s, it now has a rich development in Christian contexts as a grounded source of strength for the people: *sumud* functions as an umbrella term for many ideas. It means being connected to the Palestinian land, to home, and to daily life. It symbolises the value of a "peaceful life under the olive tree", as well as appreciating the beauty and joy of life. But *sumud* also points to broader causes and to the community's struggle. It can express willingness to sacrifice and suffer if need be, and calls on Palestinians to stay resilient like a cactus in the desert.

1. The spirituality of *sumud* brings together many of the aspects of a *praxis* of justice and reconciliation: beginning in the experience of affliction, it is nonetheless situated in relational theology seeking justice and peace. Spirituality in its simplest meaning is the life of the Spirit, embracing the human spirit, the human *zeitgeist* (spirit of the times), the energy grounding hope, itself linking with the Divine, the Universal Spirit of life that is shared by all faiths. But

the meaning of spirit that unites a struggling people in the most literal way is the Spirit as breath of life grounding hope.

2. Taking a deep breath in this Dark Night of the Palestinian people, and of many peoples in the Middle East, means, firstly, connecting with this spirit, calling on resources for the long haul, refusing to give way to the suffocating effects of daily humiliation.[23] Drawing deep on the Spirit, the breath of life, is keeping hope alive.

Secondly, taking a deep breath brings the gift of *living peacefully when there is no peace*: this means calling on a type of imagination that is prophetic in remembering and seeing differently, an imagination that summons an afflicted people to live out of a new reality that does not yet exist but can be embodied in every act of non-violent resistance, of giving thanks, giving God praise, in acts of simple kindness, moments of joy, beauty, singing, and dancing. In so doing, strength is drawn from ancient traditions that form Palestinian identity, such as hospitality, love of the beauty of the land and its culture and feasts, the myths and poems that celebrate this, and the stories that children will remember. In times of persecution, tensions, and daily harassment, it is even more important to draw strength from cherished traditions.[24]

The Lutheran pastor and theologian, Mitri Raheb, Director of an impressive educational project in Bethlehem (now in the Occupied West Bank) stresses the importance of culture for Palestinian contextual theology as well as for a spirituality of *sumud:*

> Culture becomes thus the space where people can meet others and themselves, where they can discover a language that is local yet universal, and where they realize that in order to breathe, one has to keep the windows wide open to new winds and fresh air that blow in from across the seas and oceans.[25]

Toine van Teeffelen and Fuad Giacaman of the Arab Education Institute Center in Bethlehem (AEI) see the importance of *sumud* for a theology and spirituality of non-violent resistance. Historically, in 1978 the term was given to a fund in Jordan that collected contributions from Arab countries to support the conditions of Palestinians in the occupied territories. Since then it has passed through several meanings and has come to symbolise the value of staying put while confronting an overwhelmingly stronger military and political force. Raja Shehadeh, a lawyer from Ramallah, has giving the concept two important meanings: roughly speaking, an exterior and an interior interpretation. On the one hand, the *samid* or "steadfast one" refuses to accept being dominated by the occupation; on the other, he or she refuses to become dominated by feelings of revenge and hatred of the enemy. Yet the advocating of "staying put, [of the] refusal to leave the land" should be seen as more as imaginative resistance, challenging the spirit to move on, "crossing boundaries along alternate routes, despite pains and sacrifices".[26] This is reminiscent of the New Testament context where Jesus, who, in his own context of Occupation (in this case, the Roman army in Judea), when warning his followers of the great persecutions that are to come, tells them not to fear:

> Not a hair of your head shall be destroyed: *through your unflinching endurance* you will take possession of your lives.[27]

Perhaps the most significant dimension of the spirituality of *sumud* is the dimension of vision. All the writers cited so far are eloquent in their hopes for a land shared peacefully between two peoples, for an end to occupation and the sharing of Jerusalem. They call on a vision of the Holy Spirit as beauty to sustain this hope and the reality of struggle.[28] Beauty is linked with the holy and the truthful, and possesses a unique power to move hearts. The challenge for the moral imagination of a theology of non-violence is to transcend narrow, deadlocked views, while still living amidst cycles of violence, building on people's participation, and the creating of spaces for authentic and renewed relationships of trust. To be steadfast and resilient, there is need for a disciplined spiritual practice—Gandhi saw that this was crucial and tried to put it into practice in his own ashram—one that respects both the depth of woundedness at a psychic level but also the need for daily strength just to survive. Hence emerges the call for a new understanding of the Spirit in the context of this affliction.

The Spirit as encounter, as go-between, as reconciler

The person who first set me off on a quest for new dimensions of the Holy Spirit in 1972 was the late Bishop of Winchester, John Taylor, who wrote a much-loved book called *The Go-Between God*.[29] In this work Taylor developed an inspirational theology of the Holy Spirit as the energy or force-field drawing people together in relation to one another. He used the word *annunciation* to express the relational encounter of mutuality—inspired by the New Testament Annunciation story (Luke 1.26–38; in another work, I recast this idea as "epiphanies of connection" because I think this expression better captures the idea of mutual encounter).[30] It was Taylor who first pointed me to the Jewish thinker Martin Buber as inspiration for "I and Thou" mutuality, and his insistence on "In the beginning was the Relation", instead of the more Scriptural "in the Beginning was the Word", from the Prologue of John's Gospel. Buber's call for the mutuality of the Word was a leitmotif that US theologian Carter Heyward then developed in her ground-breaking book *The Redemption of God* in 1982.[31] Since these early days there has been great cloud of witnesses as to the empowering dynamics of Relational Theology in Feminist theology, and beyond. Many will agree that the ideas of mutuality, connection, compassion, wisdom, relation, and relational justice have continued to inspire and sustain many movements for justice.

A key connection that I pursue specifically in this context of affliction is that God is our very passion for justice and at the heart of faith. Justice—the concern of both Job and Jesus—is at the heart of faith because the concern for justice is fuelled by God's very self. It is not an optional add-on. Justice could be considered as the very heartbeat of God. As Carter Heyward wrote:

> In the beginning, long before there was any idea of God, something stirred. In that cosmic moment pulsating with possibility, God breathed into space and, groaning in passion and pain and hope, gave birth to creation. We cannot remember this easily, for we cannot easily bear to remember the pain and hope of our own beginning. But it was good.[32]

In the beginning was God. In the beginning was relation, because God *is* the power and energy of our relating, our yearning for justice and right relation. Whether we speak about God's creation of the universe, the embodying of Jesus to heal the broken connections, or the wind and flame of the Spirit at Pentecost birthing communities of connection, we are speaking of God's passion for justice, for healed relationships among all people, all the creatures of the Earth. If the Divine purpose for Creation is a healed and restored universe (traditional theology calls it *reconciliation*), justice and peace are the paths to achieving this. These are pre-conditions for reconciliation. Our passion for justice confronts the fact that though we yearn for mutuality and connectedness, broken, fractured relation is in fact what surrounds, even overwhelms, us on personal, community, and international levels. And nowhere today is this seen more clearly than in the Middle East.

Thus the work of the Spirit, the great Reconciler, is the re-making of broken connections, the restoration, no less, of the vivifying energy of Creation. And it is the Spirit as catalyst for Restorative Justice that seeks to transform the corrupt systems that are in place, to find breakthroughs in interpersonal and intergroup conflict. Rooted in older traditions of community justice, Restorative Justice is continually inspired by the Sermon on the Mount, and by earlier biblical concepts like Jubilee (a year of freedom, restoration, and forgiveness)[33] and *shalom* (from Hebrew) or *salaam* (from Arabic), meaning "peace with justice".

In seeking right relationships, not vengeance, restorative justice refocuses our gaze. Is it the state or the person whose body, soul, or property was violated? What is real accountability? Is it "taking your punishment", or "taking responsibility for restoring right relation as far as possible"? Can a people who have been violated and oppressed "forgive and forget"? Or does true healing and reconciliation require, as I have argued, remembering, truth-telling, repenting, and forgiving? For restorative justice, the key is to move away from an adversarial approach and, through factors like truth-telling, mutual repentance, and a reconciling process, to aim for healing for all parties in a given situation. On an international level, this comes into play strikingly where governments tell the truth about atrocities carried out in the name of the state. So, during the past twenty-five years, there have been more than twenty Truth Commissions around the world, with the best known example being the Truth and Reconciliation Commission (TRC) of South Africa in which Archbishop Desmond Tutu played such a prominent part. As the Archbishop noted at the Apartheid Tribunal of South Africa in 1981, "Without memory, there is no healing. Without forgiveness, there is no future".[34] Far more recently there has been a move by the British government to apologize and compensate for atrocities against the Mau-Mau in Kenya in the colonial era. The call for reconciliation is a very real one for our times.

But I want to look at something far more complex than the one-to-one restoration of right relation between individuals, or even on a national basis, namely justice for the Biblical lands of the Middle East. In these places, to speak of God today is, for Christians, to utter those cries of affliction that still emerge from the Ayacuchos of the world, desperate appeals to the compassion of the international community to help them to stay resilient, vulnerable, and responsive to the guidance of the Reconciling Spirit. Just as the first Christians, terrified after the Crucifixion of Jesus, were energised by this Spirit of fire at Pentecost to begin proclaiming the message of peace with justice, so too must the modern faithful be invigorated by the Spirit of Peace.

And to begin this journey, we take the road to Gaza with one of the earliest missionary disciples, the deacon Philip.

Notes

1. Simone Weil, *Waiting on God: The Essence of Her Thought*, Emma Crauford (trans.) (London: Collins Fount Paperbacks, 1977), p. 43 and p. 76.
2. Gustavo Gutiérrez, "How can God be discussed from the perspective of Ayacucho?", in *On the Threshold of the Third Millennium, Concilium* (1990/1), pp. 103–114.
3. Ibid., pp. 107–108.
4. The Biennial Conference organised by Bethlehem Bible College, "Christ at the Checkpoint", is an expression of this hope. The latest event was in March 2014.

5. Image taken from Wikimedia Commons, <http://commons.wikimedia.org/wiki/File:Simone_Weil_1921.jpg>.
6. See her biography by David McLellan, *Simone Weil: Utopian Pessimist* (Oxford: Palgrave Macmillan, 1989).
7. For on-going, up-to-date news and reflection on this, see *Cornerstone*, the publication of Sabeel Ecumenical Liberation Centre, Jerusalem; <http://www.sabeel.org>. Also, Gideon Levy, *The Punishment of Gaza* (London: Verso, 2010).
8. Simone Weil, "The Love of God and Affliction", in Crauford, Ema (trans.), *Waiting on God: The Essence of Her Thought*, pp. 76–7.
9. Ibid., p. 80.
10. Ibid.
11. Gustavo Gutiérrez, *On Job: God-talk and the suffering of the Innocent* (New York, Maryknoll: Orbis, 1989).
12. This Biblical passage, Job 24.2–14, is taken from Gutiérrez, *On Job*, p. 33. His quotations are taken from the The New Jerusalem Bible, (London: Darton, Longman and Todd, 1985).
13. See Colin South's reflections in this in connection with Israel/Palestine: "Accepting the Fact of Death, We are freed to live more fully", in Leonard Harrow (ed.), *Living Stones Yearbook 2012* (London: Living Stones of the Holy Land Trust, 2012), pp. 120–142.
14. Gutiérrez, "How can God be discussed?", p. 108. Johan Baptist Metz was a German-born Liberation Theologian who was an enormous influence on the development of Liberation Theology. Bartolomé De Los Casas is a hero for Gustavo Gutiérrez. He was a sixteenth-century Spanish historian, social reformer, and Dominican friar. He became the first resident Bishop of Chiapas, Mexico, and the first officially appointed "Protector of the Indians"; see Gustavo Gutiérrez, *Los Casas: In search of the Poor of Jesus Christ* (New York, Maryknoll: Orbis, 1993).
15. I refer to the present policies of the Israeli government, not to the history of the conflict which originates in nineteenth-century Zionism, the Balfour Declaration (1917), and the years of the British Mandate in Palestine. See <http://www.balfourproject.org>.
16. Ilan Pappé, *The Forgotten Palestinians: A History of the Palestinians in Israel* (Yale: Yale University Press, 2011).
17. UN Resolution 194, 11 December 1948.

18. See Ilan Pappé, *The Ethnic Cleansing of the Palestinians* (Oxford: Oneworld, 2006).
19. Ibid., pp. 236–237.
20. Ibid., pp. 225–234.
21. Philippe Gaillard, "Memory never forgets Miracles", in Carol Rittner *et al* (eds.), *Genocide in Rwanda: Complicity of the Churches* (St Paul, MN: Paragon House, 2004), p. 111.
22. For example, Saffuriya (Roman Sepphoris) was renamed as Hebrew Zippori.
23. See Grey, *The Advent of Peace*, pp. 84–87.
24. See Mary Grey, "Taking a Deep Breath: Spiritual Resources for a Pedagogy of Hope", in Toine van Teeffelen (ed.), *Challenging the Wall: toward a Pedagogy of Hope* (Bethlehem: Arab Education Institute Center, 2008), pp. 9–10.
25. Mitri Raheb, "Culture as the art to Breathe", <http://www.annadwa.org/news/newsletter_sep06.htm>; also, *idem*, "Culture as the art of breathing", in van Teeffelen (ed.), *Challenging the Wall*, p. 18.
26. Toine van Teeffelen and Fuad Giacaman, "Sumud: Resistance in Daily Life", in van Teeffelen(ed.), *Challenging the Wall*, p. 30.
27. Luke 21.18–19; Matthew 10.22.
28. This will be explored and developed in Chapter 6.
29. John V. Taylor, *The Go-Between God* (London: Collins, 1972).
30. See Mary Grey, *The Wisdom of Fools? Seeking Revelation for Today* (London: SPCK, 1993).
31. Isobel Carter Heyward, *The Redemption of God: A Theology of Relation* (Washington DC: Washington Square Press, 1982).
32. Carter Heyward, *Our Passion for Justice*, (Cleveland: The Pilgrim Press, 1984), p. 25.
33. See Leviticus 25.1–4, 8–10.
34. See <http://robt.shepherd.tripod.com/tutu.html>. For a longer exploration see Desmond Tutu, *No Future without Forgiveness* (New York: Random House, 1999).

CHAPTER 2

Gaza in history and in contemporary reality

Then an angel of the Lord said to Philip, "Get up, and go toward the south to the road that goes down from Jerusalem to Gaza".

Acts 8.26

Your Holiness, Pope Francis,

At Christmas, as you say, we contemplate "the faithfulness and tenderness" of Boundless Love. This holiday also embraces the season of refugees recalling The Holy Family's flight to Egypt to escape Herod's massacre of the innocents. Their journey from Bethlehem meant passing through Gaza, which, since 1948, is itself in a wretched refugee limbo. Families in Gaza have no escape. Its borders are hermetically sealed and bound by Israel and Egypt. *Gaza needs your help.*

***Dr Vacy Vlazna,* Gaza calling: A Christmas appeal to Pope Francis *(emphasis is mine)*[1]**

The Gentile Pentecost

On the journey that this book will follow, everything began in Jerusalem—but will not end there. It was in Jerusalem that the terrified apostles and disciples were empowered by the Holy Spirit and began to do what Jesus had commanded: "Go into all the world and proclaim the good news to the whole creation!" (Mark 16.15). It is Jerusalem that will always draw Christians and Jews back to their roots. But the dynamism of the Spirit will never remain tied by geographical boundaries. And it is precisely the Spirit's dynamic revelation of the *universality* of mission that is the guiding light for this book's journey. This was the revelation that was given to Peter while he was staying at Simon the Tanner's house at the ancient port of Joppa (Acts 10; tanning was considered as an unclean occupation by the Jews). Here in this old port Peter received a visit from three men sent by Cornelius, a devout and loyal Roman centurion from Caesarea—a city which also lay by the sea—begging him to accompany them to Cornelius's house. (Caesarea will become significant for Paul later in our story).

What makes this tale significant for the direction of early Christianity is that Peter had just received a vision of "all kinds of four-footed animals, reptiles, and birds of the air" and a command to "kill and eat" (Acts 10.12–13), a command which he had initially refused (Acts 10.14) as this meant eating creatures which Jews considered to be unclean. The voice said to him: "What God has cleansed, you must not call common" (Acts 10.15).What this vision is revealing to Peter is that the Gospel of Jesus was meant for all nations, and he has to unlearn his rigid understanding of the categories of purity and what is clean or unclean. As the US theologian Nancy Victorin-Vangerud writes:

> Luke associates the Spirit in the Gentile Pentecost with the work of confronting particular cultural values and practices toward "retrieving" a new inclusive humanity . . . God the Spirit communicates a new orientation creating a universal identity for the Jesus movement.[2]

This new inclusive humanity is an integral part of the intention of New Testament writers, especially Luke; as Peter proclaims the Good News of Jesus at Caesarea, the Holy Spirit falls on all those present—"even on the Gentiles" (Acts 10.45)—and Cornelius and his household baptized in the name of Christ. The crucial message here is that the privileging of the Jerusalem Pentecost must not be allowed to obscure the Gentile Pentecost at Joppa and Caesarea and the blessing of new identity by Christian Baptism conferred on people often rejected, ridiculed, or considered of a lower status.

The Spirit leads Philip

But let us not begin with the more famous journeys of Peter, John, or Paul but, rather, with a comparatively little-known figure, the deacon and evangelist Philip (not to be confused with the apostle Philip from Bethsaida whom we would recognize particularly from the Gospel of John, chapters 14–16). This Philip was one of the seven Greek-speaking men selected by the apostles to distribute food and alms to the widows and poor of Jerusalem (Acts 6.1–7). His journey begins at a poignant moment in the history of the fledgling Christian community—truly the time of affliction foretold by Jesus. The apostles had already been flung into prison; Stephen, one of the seven chosen as deacons, would become the first martyr of the new faith when he was stoned to death (Acts 7.54–60). In the background of this cruel event stood Saul (whose Latin name was Paul)[3] who began to destroy the church: "But Saul was ravaging the Church by entering house after house; dragging off both men and women he committed them to prison" (Acts 8.3).

Enter Philip, at this *kairos* moment.[4] First, Philip went to a city in Samaria to preach the Gospel (Acts 8.5), converting the people there from the witchcraft of Simon Magus. Simon himself is said to have been one of the converts whom Philip baptized (Acts 8.13). Then, inspired by an angel (which I understand to mean as being empowered by the Spirit), he was told (Acts 8.26):

> Then an angel from the Lord said to Philip, "Get up, and go toward the south to the road that goes down from Jerusalem to Gaza."

This command—highlighting the centrality of the role of the Spirit—is illustrative of the whole theology of Acts. For Luke (who is assumed to be the writer of Acts), this is now the time of the Spirit, the Pentecost of the Gentiles as well as that of the Jews, just as his Gospel was the time of Jesus.[5] *The fire and energy of the Holy Spirit is what transforms a situation of affliction and persecution into a time of hope.*

Philip's encounter in his travels south to Gaza has become famous, especially as we trace the beginnings of Christianity in Northern Africa. For Philip encountered—again under the guidance of the Spirit—an Ethiopian eunuch, a servant of the Queen of Ethiopia who happened to be reading the passage in Isaiah about the suffering servant (Isaiah 53.4–11, vv. 7–8 in particular). We can only conjecture as to the connections this man was making with his own suffering. As the story relates, Philip baptized him and they both went on their way. Presumably, the eunuch returned to Ethiopia, and thereafter was born the Christian faith in that part of Africa to where he returned.

As for Philip, he now travelled as a missionary, preaching in every city from Azotus (Ashdod, a city of the Philistines) northwards to Caesarea, where he and his four daughters, who were known as prophets, established a home. It was there that he would receive the Apostle Paul (Acts 21). We do not know if he ever reached further into Gaza; he may not even have arrived there, but Christianity did eventually appear in that region and flourished in many different ways. Gaza now becomes the next step of this journey.

Gaza—ancient city with a rich history

Gaza—sometimes referred to as Gaza City—is an ancient Palestinian city in the Gaza Strip with a population of about 450,000; it is the largest city in the Palestinian territories.[6] Inhabited since at least the fifteenth century BC, Gaza has been dominated by several different peoples and empires throughout its history. The Philistines made it a part of their *pentapolis* after the Ancient Egyptians had ruled it for nearly 350 years.[7] It was here that the Biblical Samson was imprisoned after his eyes had been gouged out by the Philistines: as the famous story tells it, he eventually killed himself and his persecutors by bringing down the house upon them all (Judges 16.23–31). The beginnings of Christianity in Gaza are uncertain—was it around the time of Philip? What is certain is that for a long time Christianity was not widely accepted by its people.

Though Christianity already had an uneasy presence in the community for more than two hundred years, Constantine the Great (AD 272–337) forcibly introduced the new faith into Gaza; such was the hostility of the pagan population that Bishop Asclepas deemed it wise to build the church outside the city. The first church built in Gaza itself was the work of St Irenion (d. 393). While Gaza experienced relative peace and the flourishing of its port under the Romans, and later the Byzantines, the inhabitants of Gaza continually fought against Christianity. As the historian Martin Meyer explains:

> The first Christian martyr of Gaza whose name is known is the bishop Sylvanus, who met his death in 285. In 293, the ninth year of Diocletian, persecutions of the Christians broke out afresh; in the following year, Timotheus, Agapus, and Thecla suffered martyrdom at Gaza; and in the same year, Alexander, a young Christian of the city, was beheaded at Caesarea for professing his faith. In 299 the Christians who had assembled at Gaza to hear the Scriptures read were seized and mutilated; and from 302 to 310 persecutions were continuous throughout the Roman Empire.[8]

Under the Emperor Julian (also known as the Apostate, r. 361–363), Christians suffered severe persecution.[9] Three brothers, Eusebius, Nestabos, and Zeno, were put to death at Gaza by the populace. As is clear, Gaza was stubborn in its opposition to Christianity (although, at this time Gaza was not alone in persecuting Christians: similar acts of suppression were also happening in Lebanon and Syria).

In 395 came the turning point in the Christian history of Gaza with the arrival of its new bishop, St Porphyry (d. 420), known as the true restorer of Christianity in Gaza. This sainted bishop first sent Mark, his deacon and historian, to Constantinople to obtain an order to close the pagan temples. The Christians then scarcely numbered 200 in Gaza,[10] though the rest of the empire was gradually abandoning its idols. After two attempts at petitioning governmental authorities—along with an accurate prophecy that the empress would bear a son—the pagan temples of Gaza were permitted to be destroyed, with the exception of the Marneion, the temple sacred to Zeus Marnas, which had replaced that of Dagon. There was no great change, however, in the sentiments of the people, so St Porphyry decided to strike a decisive blow. He went himself to Constantinople during the winter of 401–402 and obtained from the Byzantine Emperor Arcadius a decree for the destruction of the pagan temples, which Cynegius, a special imperial envoy, executed in May 402. Eight temples, those of Aphrodite, Hecate, the Sun, Apollo, Core, Fortune, the Heroeion, and even the Marneion, were either pulled down or burnt. Simultaneously, soldiers visited every house, seizing and burning the idols and books of magic. On the ruins of the Marneion was erected, at the expense of the empress, a large cruciform church called the Eudoxiana in her honour, and dedicated on 14 April 407. Paganism had thus ceased to exist officially.[11] The reigns of Anastasius I (399–401) and Justinian (527–565) were prosperous for Gaza. Under the leadership of Bishop Marcianus, old buildings were restored and new ones built. The dedication of new buildings provided an opportunity for lavish festivals. Theatres were active with the speeches of scholars and rhetoricians. As Meyer wrote:

> In this way the new faith took over the outer trappings of the old cult, and wrought all the forces of the life and culture of the times to its own advancement and stability.[12]

Gaza also produced many Christian scholars of high repute and—as well as Egypt—contributed to the rise of early monasticism. For example, St Hilarion was born in the village of Thawatha (near the present Tel-el-Tineh) in 291. He returned after some years to live the life of a hermit.[13] Many others were attracted to this place and a colony of hermits grew up around him. Abba Esaias (d. 489) lived in this area in complete seclusion except for his Egyptian disciple, Peter. Seridos founded a *cenobium* (a monastery where monks live in close community) about 500. It was here that the revered Barsanufius came from Egypt, later to be joined by his close friend, John the Prophet. One of the monks was Dorotheos of Gaza who had once been associated with the school of Gaza; he achieved the role of archimandrite and wrote a number of discourses in which he merged scripture and the philosophical teachings of overcoming the passions and living the virtuous life.[14]

After this era of flourishing, Gaza became the first city in Palestine to be conquered by the Rashidun army in 635,[15] and quickly developed into a centre of Islamic law. However, by the time the Crusaders invaded the city in the late eleventh century, it was in ruins. In later centuries, Gaza experienced several hardships—from Mongol raids to floods and locusts. So, sadly, it was reduced to a village by the sixteenth century, by which time it had been incorporated into the Ottoman Empire. During the first half of Ottoman rule, the Ridwan dynasty, the most prominent *pasha* family in Palestine,[16] dominated Gaza, where its members became hereditary governors. Under their rule, the city experienced an age of great commerce and peace. The municipality of Gaza was established in 1893.

Gaza was conquered by British forces during World War I, later becoming a part of the British Mandate of Palestine. As a result of the 1948 Arab-Israeli War (called, as noted previously, the *al Nakba*, "catastrophe", by the Palestinians), this community of only 80,000 was suddenly inflated by the influx of 250,000 refugees. Egypt then administered the newly formed "Gaza Strip". Gaza was captured by Israel in the Six-Day War in 1967; this meant that thousands more people were driven to refugee camps, as they had already been in 1948. In 1993, the city was transferred to the Palestinian National Authority. Hamas won the 2006 general election, which international observers considered free and fair, and formed a unity government in which MPs from Fatah and other parties were offered ministerial posts. However, in June 2006 Israeli troops abducted and jailed dozens of Hamas ministers and parliamentarians, while the US and other western governments joined Israel in refusing to recognise or speak to Hamas.

Israel and the US encouraged Fatah to stage a coup in Gaza, but Hamas pre-empted this in June 2007.The election of Hamas has meant that Gaza became a pariah state as regards the international community. In June 2010, Egypt and Israel imposed a blockade on the Gaza Strip. Israel eased the blockade allowing consumer goods, and Egypt reopened the Rafah border crossing in 2011 to pedestrians. The situation as I write—November–December 2013—is that the borders remain closed and the tunnels that the Gazan people relied on for essential food and goods are being blocked and destroyed.

This is only a brief survey of the history of this embattled strip of land: they give little clue to the present reality and level of suffering of the Gazan people in every dimension of life. As Gaza's primary economic activities are small-scale industries, agriculture, and labour, the economy has been completely devastated by the blockade and the cruelty of Israeli invasions.[17] Barest survival is under threat. Repeated reports relate that Gaza is on the brink of total collapse. "The situation in Gaza is at a point of near catastrophe," warned Richard Falk, the UN Special Rapporteur on the situation of human rights in the occupied Palestinian territories, calling for immediate intervention in Gaza to prevent a humanitarian catastrophe.[18] He stressed that lack of fuel imports has resulted in power cuts, preventing the provision of basic services including health, water, and sanitation. Power shortages have sent raw sewage flooding into the streets; the lack of water means that people are forced to buy unclean water from unregulated vendors, compounding the threats to the health of the inhabitants of Gaza. It is a small wonder that the theme of affliction is so appropriate for life in Gaza.

And what of Christianity in Gaza today? Most of the region's inhabitants are Muslim, although there is a Christian minority divided primarily among three communities: Anglican, Baptist, and Roman Catholic. Rather than relating dispassionate facts, let us try to evoke the atmosphere of Christian community life in Gaza today:

> As the sun rises in the east on the first day of Advent, the bells of Gaza's churches fill the air, mixing amicably with the Muslim call to prayer. There is an air of quiet serenity spiced with excitement as the faithful walk to their churches and mosques, the doors swinging open, and Christians and Muslims bid each other good morning on yet another Sunday.
>
> Gaza's oldest church, the Greek Orthodox St Porphyrus, dates back to the sixteenth century. The majority of Gaza's Christians are served by the Roman Catholic Church on Al Zayotoun St. and the Gaza Baptist Church, which offer living room prayer groups, interfaith outreach, several schools, and humanitarian/medical Christian charities staffed by both locals and internationals. Today Gaza is home to approximately 3,000 Christians, the majority of whom live near these Gaza City churches.[19]

Until November 1947, when the U.N. General Assembly passed Resolution 181 partitioning Palestine, Palestinian Christians lived peacefully among the Muslim and Jewish populations of the area. With the passage of the nonbinding resolution, however, Zionist forces began their ethnic cleansing campaign in earnest. At the time, Christians represented 18 per cent of Palestine's population, with many families tracing their ancestry back to the time of Christ. Today Christians comprise less than 2 per cent of Palestinians, with the loss of Jerusalem's Christian community being the most profound, plunging from a peak of 51 per cent in 1922 to just 4 per cent today.

> After 1967, along with its Muslim neighbours, Gaza's small Christian community found itself imprisoned between Israel and the sea, and the land swollen with additional refugees, as we have seen. But Gaza's Christians also discovered they

> were invisible: unacknowledged, dismissed, denounced, or forgotten by fellow Christians throughout the world, especially in the United States. Despite this global invisibility, here is a snapshot of life in the Catholic Church of the Holy Family:
>
> "Despite all the bad things you hear about Gaza, there is life here," said Father Jorge Hernandez, parish priest of Holy Family Catholic Church and Missionary of the Society of the Incarnate Word, who has been in Gaza for 2 years, "People here pray and lead virtuous lives. They are happy, even living in Gaza with all its problems: This is their homeland" he says: "Their loved ones are buried here. God is here, and it's a fruit of the Holy Spirit that people here embrace and celebrate the life they have."[20]

Of Gaza's 1.6 million people, Father Hernandez related, about 3,000 are Christian and only 206 of them are Catholics. But in a land where just about everyone is Muslim, denominations matter little:

> Most of the participants in our youth program are Orthodox. They come here to the church and I visit them in their homes. We don't worry about these things. There are many people who pray in the Orthodox church early in the morning and then come to the Catholic church for Mass. And there are quite a few of them who come just for the coffee hour. In Arab culture, that's important.[21]

A missionary of the Argentina-based religious congregation called the Institute of the Incarnate Word, Father Hernandez said the daily interactions between Christians and Gaza's Muslim majority are almost always respectful and peaceful. Yet the relationship has been tested since Hamas won the parliamentary elections in 2006 and took complete control of Gaza in 2007 (as related above). Pressure increased on Christian women to cover their heads in public. A Catholic school and convent were ransacked in 2007. Later that year, a Christian bookseller was killed and in 2008 a YMCA library was bombed. Yet Father Hernandez stated that there was no official policy against Christians, and that all Gazans were part of the same homeland, living in the same circumstances, victims of the same blockade. He described the good relations with Muslims:

> "The old people tell me how they would make a pilgrimage to Jerusalem crowded into the same car with Muslims," the priest said. "This was when the border was still open. When they got there, the Christians would go pray in church, the Muslims in the mosque, and afterward they met up and went to eat in a restaurant together. At night the families would return together to Gaza in an atmosphere of joy. There was a mutual solidarity. Muslims would come to play games at the church and stay for Mass. No one made distinctions. That was Palestinian reality. Yet today it's different, and our apostolate is to try and conserve those old values."[22]

The parish runs two schools with about 1,000 students, 90 per cent of whom are Muslims. Father Hernandez said he does not permit "even one word that lacks respect toward another's religion, whether from the Christians or from the Muslims. Anyone who violates such respect suffers immediate judgment without mercy."[23] The parish also works with youth centres on responding to Gaza's unique challenges. Father Hernandez said: "We're going to see the consequences of the occupation and blockade of Gaza long into the future. Children grow up here without the idea of their father going off to work and earning a living. The father remains in the home, because he doesn't have a job."[24] Helping young people envision a different future is part of the church's mission: "The majority of youth are working hard in the university, yet they face a future of not being able to find work. It's difficult not to be able to envision a future. These are very difficult themes. So the church is also trying to create employment opportunities, so kids can grow up with different values."[25]

Father Hernandez's predecessor, Father Manuel Musallam, was an outspoken critic of Israel's treatment of the Palestinian people. Yet, Father Musallam was Palestinian, and Father Hernandez said that, as a foreigner, he tries to maintain a more politically neutral stance. But he admits that some events have pushed him to speak out. "When the aid flotilla from

Turkey was blocked from coming here, I went to the beach to add my voice to the protest," he said. "I didn't speak specifically against Israel, but I did say that such violence only generates more violence. We're working for peace in Gaza and they made that much tougher to achieve. I had to say that. Israel will understand it however they want, as will Hamas."

Go drink the sea at Gaza!

This violent expression means "Go to Hell!" according to the Israeli journalist Amira Hass, who calls her book on the affliction of the Gazan people *Drinking the Sea in Gaza*;[26] the expression is attributed to Yitzak Rabin, a former Israeli Prime Minister. How to understand international neglect and weak response to Gazan suffering is the question. The usual reaction is to say that, because Hamas is firing rockets into Israel (in the Sderot region), the Israeli response is justified. But what a disproportionate response!

Here are the facts about the Qassam rockets: the first homemade Qassam missile was fired across the Israeli border in October 2001; the first fatality occurred in March 2007. Up to November 2008, thirteen Israelis were killed by Qassam rockets. By contrast, between September 2000 and the end of November 2008, nearly 5,000 Palestinians were killed in retaliatory strikes, more than half of them in Gaza. The rockets have, in the last year, reached more distant targets, but they are ineffectual, in military terms, when compared to the fire-power of the US F-16s, Apache helicopter gunships, Merkava tanks, and naval gunships with which Israel is equipped. Hamas say the missiles are in retaliation not only for the many deaths Israel has caused both in Gaza and the West Bank, but also for the continued occupation and expropriation of land. They say that they hope to end the occupation in this way; much as Israel was forced to end the occupation of South Lebanon by Hezbollah.[27]

What has been and is happening in Gaza is beyond all proportionate response. Here is what Noam Chomsky wrote after a visit to Gaza in November 2012 (emphasis is mine):

Even a single night in jail is enough to give a taste of what it means to be under the total control of some external force.

And it hardly takes more than a day in Gaza to appreciate what it must be like to try to survive in *the world's largest open-air prison*, where some 1.5 million people on a roughly 140-square-mile strip of land are subject to random terror and arbitrary punishment, with no purpose other than to humiliate and degrade.

Such cruelty is to ensure that Palestinian hopes for a decent future will be crushed, and rights will be nullified. The Israeli political leadership has dramatically illustrated this commitment in the past few days, warning that they will "go crazy" if Palestinian rights are given even limited recognition by the U.N.

This threat to "go crazy" ("nishtagea")—that is, launch a tough response—is deeply rooted, stretching back to the Labor governments of the 1950s, along with the related "Samson Complex": If crossed, we will bring down the Temple walls around us.

Thirty years ago, Israeli political leaders, including some noted hawks, submitted to Prime Minister Menachem Begin a shocking report on how settlers on the West Bank regularly committed "terrorist acts" against Arabs there, with total impunity.

Disgusted, the prominent military-political analyst Yoram Peri wrote that the Israeli army's task, it seemed, was not to defend the state, but "to demolish the rights of innocent people just because they are Araboushim (a harsh racial epithet) living in territories that God promised to us."

Gazans have been singled out for particularly cruel punishment. Thirty years ago, in his memoir "The Third Way," Raja Shehadeh, a lawyer, described the hopeless task of trying to protect fundamental human rights within a legal system designed to ensure failure, and his personal experience as a Samid, "a steadfast one," who watched his

> home turned into a prison by brutal occupiers and could do nothing but somehow "endure."[28]

Since then, as he has written, the situation has become much worse. The Oslo Accords made Gaza and the West Bank a single territorial entity. These negotiations were frustrated by the fact that the U.S. and Israel had already initiated their program to separate Gaza and the West Bank, so as to block a diplomatic settlement and punish inhabitants in both territories, a punishment that became severe for the Gazans in 2006, when, as I related, Hamas was elected as the ruling party of their government. That election provoked a brutal siege. When the Gazans blocked a coup attempt, there was a sharp escalation of the siege and attacks, culminating, in winter 2008–09, with Operation Cast Lead, one of the most vicious exercises of military force in recent memory: a defenseless and trapped civilian population was subjected to relentless attack by one of the world's most advanced military organisations, an assault reliant on U.S. arms and protected by U.S. diplomacy.

Of course, it is always argued, there had to be Israeli pretexts for such a vicious attack. The usual one, as I have already hinted at, is "security": in this case, the security issue was the homemade rockets launched from Gaza. Gideon Levy, journalist with Ha'Arets in Jerusalem, points out the emptiness of this claim:

> Israel is causing electricity blackouts; laying sieges; bombing and shelling; assassinating and imprisoning; killing and wounding civilians, including children and babies, in horrifying numbers—but "they started it."[29]

Levy points out that Israel's disengagement from Gaza in 2005 did nothing to change the living conditions of the people resident there and the reality of its being a vast prison. It needs to be understood that Israel still controls Gaza's water supply, electricity, and means of communication. In fact Israel controls the life and death of its people: they are prevented from seeking urgent medical aid in Egypt, or indeed anywhere.

Gideon Levy asks, if Hamas had not fired rockets, would Israel have lifted the economic siege? "Nonsense!" he says,[30] and admits that the violence actually began during the Israeli occupation—and there is no violence worse than the violence of an occupier. Even the question, "Who started it?" is an evasion distorting the whole picture. This is what the international community needs to look at: the entire context of the situation and the barbaric cruelty that Israel continues to inflict on Gaza.

Refugee camps in Gaza

The bare facts relate a story of human affliction: Jabalia Camp, located north of Gaza City, was established after the 1948 Arab-Israeli conflict for 35,000 refugees who had fled from villages in southern Palestine. They were first provided with tents, a temporary solution which the United Nations Relief and Works Agency (UNRWA) later replaced with cement block shelters with asbestos roofs. Beach Camp, known locally as "Shati Camp", lies beside the sea in the northern part of Gaza City, and was established on 747 dunums[31] (less than one square kilometre) after the 1948 conflict for some 23,000 refugees from Lydda, Jaffa, Beersheva, and the southern coastal plain of Palestine. Nuseirat Camp is eight kilometres south of Gaza City, and is named after a local Bedouin tribe. About 16,000 refugees settled in the camp after the 1948 Arab-Israeli conflict, most having fled from the Beersheva area in the Negev in southern Palestine. Many were housed initially in a former British military prison (Kallaboush) and others were sheltered in tents. The poorest section of the camp is known as the "new camp" or Block J. Bureij Camp, set up in 1949 on a 528 dunum site, is located in the centre of the Gaza Strip to the east of the Salah Eddin main road. A number of the original 13,000 refugees were housed in the British army barracks there, while the rest had to endure living in tents. UNRWA built cement block shelters here in the 1950s. Maghazi (or Meghazi) Camp, situated in the centre of the Gaza Strip south of Bureij camp, was established in 1949 on a 559 dunum site to shelter 9,000 refugees who had fled from villages in central and southern Palestine. Tents were replaced by mud-brick shelters in the 1950s, and later by cement block shelters in the 1960s. Deir el-Balah camp is the smallest camp in the Gaza Strip, covering an area of 160,000 sq. meters, lying beside the sea in the middle of the Gaza Strip and west of the town of Deir el-Balah ("Monastery of Dates"). The area is well-known for its abundant date palm groves. Khan Younis Camp is located about two kilometres from the sea in the south of the Gaza Strip, and was established in 1949 west of Khan Younis City, a major commercial centre which was historically a stopping-off point on the ancient trade route to Egypt. The original 35,000 residents, most of them from villages in the Beersheva area in the Negev, were, at first, housed in tents on a 549 dunum site. Rafah Camp, located on the Egyptian border, is the southern-most camp. The camp was established in 1949 to house 41,000 refugees. At that time it was the largest and most concentrated population of refugees in the Gaza Strip. However, several thousand residents have since moved from the camp to a housing project in nearby Tel es-Sultan.

In summary, there are eight refugee camps in Gaza with 393,000 people living in them, 55 per cent of the total number of refugees in the region, "The rest of the refugees, about 320,000 people, have been scattered throughout Gaza's old and new residential neighbourhoods".[32] It is women who define camp life, wrote Sara Roy:

> It is women who sleep with six or seven in one room; who trudge daily through mud roads to local markets; who, for hours on end, collect water from dripping faucets after the main lines have been shut down, and who perpetually scrub shelters under constant assault by sand and dust. The men are cleaning streets in Tel Abiv and Askelon, spending their nights there in shacks illegally padlocked by their Israeli employers.[33]

Surviving in the midst of affliction

This story of suffering and affliction can never presume to totally define a people. I have related how Christian communities try to keep joy and hope alive through the rhythm of faith and life. This goes beyond the boundaries of faith to embrace all the people. Witness to the way the Spirit keeps hope alive in the Gazan people, who, in spite of the severity of camp life—the lack of sewage disposal, the restricted water supply (and only brackish water at that), and the ruin of the infrastructure of their lives due to the Israeli incursions—continue to feed their children, send them to school, and maintain the dignity of life. Amira Hass relates this ability to sustain dignity during a visit:

> I quickly forget the oppressive dinginess of the Khan Yunis camp when the older children somehow find a space—at the table, on the floor, leaning over a chair—to concentrate on their books even as the adults' conversation swirls around them. They are not distracted by talk of the elections and campaigns, about a particular candidate's rally where people asked difficult question. They ignore their parents' boasting about their good grades. The poverty seems far away when Kauthar, having taught school all day, nursed her infant son, fed her other two children, and baked thirty-seven pitas, sits down to pore over Hamlet for a course at the Islamic University, "because life cannot just be food and children."[34]

This is *sumud* (referred to in Chapter 1), steadfastness and resilience in the face of affliction. *Sumud* as daily practice. *Sumud* also manifested as heroism, given the courage shown by many doctors, nurses, and aid workers during Israeli incursions as they tried to rescue people trapped under rubble, or children traumatised by the war situation. But *sumud* manifested also by the extraordinary ability to forgive across the ethnic boundaries. To illustrate the capacity of unfettered forgiveness, I end this chapter with the story of the Gazan doctor Dr Izzeldin Abuelaish. His story manifests freedom from fear and a refusal to hate that demonstrates the dynamism of the Holy Spirit's energy of peace-making.

On 16 January 2009 three Palestinian sisters were killed when an Israeli tank fired two shells into their bedroom. They were the daughters of a Palestinian gynaecologist, who, uniquely for a Gazan doctor, held a consultant post in an Israeli hospital. Abuelaish's book, *I Shall Not Hate*,[35] is an account of his life up to this momentous event, movingly explaining his remarkable reaction. In essence, Abuelaish, who likens hate to disease and communication to cure, has drawn on his medical experience to seek a new approach to the resolution of apparently insoluble conflict.[36]

Minutes after the attack, Abuelaish telephoned his friend, the Israeli Channel 10 News journalist Shlomi Eldar, to ask for help:

> By chance, Eldar was live on air. There then followed what must surely qualify as one of the most distressing interviews ever broadcast. We watch the face of the seasoned Israeli anchorman slowly collapse, as the news of the disaster is relayed to him by his Palestinian friend. Eldar holds out his mobile, switched to speaker phone, as Abuelaish's screams of despair ring out.[37]

In reaction to this event, international condemnation of the Israel incursion escalated and it finally ended forty-eight hours later. What is important is the way that Abuelaish refused to give way to hatred (his wife had recently died of leukaemia just before the Israeli incursion). Realising that "violence begets violence and breeds more hatred," Abuelaish learned Hebrew, developing what he believes to be the key skill of an effective doctor: communication.[38] Now able to communicate directly with both Jews and Arabs, Abuelaish found that "they feel as I do: we are more similar than we are different, and we are all fed up with violence."[39] His book concludes with his realisation that his greatest personal and professional challenge still remains: to cure the disease of hatred. He does not deny the anger he feels about what has happened to him; instead, he conducts it into a radical "immunisation programme," which, as he puts it, will inject people "with respect, dignity, and equality," one that will inoculate them "against hatred."

At this moment of hope it is time to take to the road again, this time with Paul to Damascus.

Notes

1. Vacy Vlazna, "Gaza calling: A Christmas appeal to Pope Francis", from Aljazeera (23 December 2013), <http://www.aljazeera.com/indepth/opinion/2013/12/gaza-calling-christmas-appeal-pope-francis-201312221232347236 6.html>.
2. Nancy M. Victorin-Vangerud, *The Raging Hearth: Spirit in the Household of God* (Missouri: Chalice Press, 2000), p. 191.
3. It is frequently, and incorrectly, assumed that Saul received his new name after his conversion. It was quite usual for Roman citizens to have two names: an "official" name for the purposes of Roman administration and a personal name.
4. It is interesting that the deacons, at least Philip and Stephen, had interpreted their roles as being much wider than distributing food to the widows and poor. A "*kairos* moment" is a decisive moment in history.
5. The theology of Luke differs from the theology of John. For John, the Risen Jesus gives the Spirit (John 20.19, 21). For Luke it is the event of Pentecost (Acts 2).
6. See <http://en.wikipedia.org/wiki/Gaza>.
7. A *pentapolis* is a group of five cities: in the case of the Philistines they were Ashkelon, Ashdod, Ekron, Gath, and Gaza
8. Martin A. Meyer, *History of the City of Gaza: From the Earliest Times to the Present Day* (New York: Columbia University Press, 1907), p. 60.
9. As related by the fifth century historian Sozomen, himself very influenced by the miracles of Hilarion. See Sozomen, *History of the Church in Nine Books* (London: Samuel Bagster and Sons, 1846), vol. 5, pp. 220–221.
10. There is roughly the same number of Roman Catholics today.
11. Mark the Deacon, *Life of Porphyry*, (Oxford: Oxford Clarendon Press, 1913).
12. Meyer, *History of the City of Gaza.*, p. 67.
13. Sad to relate, St Hilarion was later compelled to flee to Sicily to escape persecution by the pagans; as told by Sozomen, *History of the Church*, vol. 5, pp. 220–221.
14. Peter Brown, "The Rise and Function of the Holy Man in Late Antiquity", *Journal of Roman Studies*, vol. 61 (1971), pp. 80–100.

15. The Rashidun Caliphate Army or *Rashidun army* was the primary military body of the Rashidun Caliphate's armed forces during the Muslim conquests of the seventh century, serving alongside the Rashidun Navy. It maintained a high level of discipline, strategic prowess, and organization.
16. *Pasha* was a higher rank in the Ottoman Empire political and military system, typically granted to governors, generals, dignitaries, and others.
17. Most of Gaza's inhabitants are Muslim, although there is a Christian minority. Gaza has a very young population with roughly 75 per cent under the age of 25. The city is currently administered by a 14-member municipal council.
18. Richard Falk, "The Latest Gaza Catastrophe: Will They Ever Learn?", from his blog *Global Justice in the 21st Century* (20 November 2013), <http://richardfalk.wordpress.com/2012/11/18/the-latest-gaza-catastrophe-will-they-ever-learn/>; this is an update of Falk, "The latest Gaza catastrophe", Aljazeera (18 November 2012), <http://www.aljazeera.com/indepth/opinion/2012/11/2012111874429224963.html>.
19. Mohammad Omer, "Gaza's Christian Community—Serenity, Solidarity and Soulfulness", *The Washington Report on Middle Eastern Affairs* (January-February, 2008), p. 16.
20. Paul Jeffrey, "Gaza church nurtures hope despite Israeli blockade and Hamas control", Catholic News Service (22 February 2011), <http://www.catholicnews.com/data/stories/cns/1100730.htm>.
21. Ibid.
22. Ibid.
23. Ibid.
24. Ibid.
25. Ibid.
26. Amira Hass, *Drinking the Sea at Gaza: Days and Nights in a Land under Siege*, Elana Wesley and Maxine Kaufman-Lacusta (trans.) (New York: Holt Paperback, 1996). Copyright © 1996 by Amira Hass. Translated by Elana Wesley and Maxine Kaufman-Lacusta. Translation copyright © 1999 by Metropolitan Books. Reprinted by permission of Henry Holt and Company, LLC. All rights reserved.
27. See <http://www.foa.org.uk/news/facts-about-gaza>. Also <http://www.palestinecampaign.org>, <http://www.ochaopt.org>, <http://www.btselem.org>, <http://www.amnesty.org.uk>, <http://www.christianaid.org.uk>,

<http://www.savethechildren.org.uk>, <http://www.adalah.org>, and <http://www.icahd.org>.

28. Noam Chomsky, "My Visit to Gaza, the World's Largest Open-Air Prison", *Truth-Out* (4 November 2012), <http://www.chomsky.info/articles/20121104.htm>.
29. Gideon Levy, *The Punishment of Gaza* (London: Verso, 2010), p. 19.
30. Ibid., p. 20.
31. The dunum is a unit of land area used in the Ottoman Empire and representing the amount of land that can be ploughed in a day.
32. Amira Hass, *Drinking the Sea at Gaza*, p. 171.
33. Sara Roy, *A Failing Peace: Gaza and the Israeli-Palestinian Conflict* (London: Pluto Press, 2007), p. 55. <http://www.plutobooks.com>.
34. Amira Hass, *Drinking the Sea at Gaza*, p. 172.
35. Izzeldin Abuelaish, *I Shall not Hate: A Gaza Doctor's journey on the Road to Peace and Human Dignity* (London: Bloomsbury, 2011).
36. See Ian McClure's review of this book, "A cure for the disease of hate" in BMJ (14 September 2011), <http://www.bmj.com/content/343/bmj.d5715>. The citation is taken from this review.
37. Abuelaish, *I Shall not Hate*, p. 101.
38. Ibid., p. 101.
39. Ibid., p. 197.

CHAPTER 3

Syria, the Arab world's broken heart

> Brother Saul, the Lord Jesus who appeared to you on the road by which you came, has sent me that you may regain your sight and be filled with the Holy Spirit.
>
> ***Acts 9.17***

> . . . No recorded event occurred in the world but Damascus was in existence to receive news of it. Go back as far as you will into the vague past, there was always a Damascus . . . She has looked upon the dry bones of a thousand empires and will see the tombs of a thousand more before she dies.
>
> ***Mark Twain,* The Innocents Abroad**[1]

Paul,[2] the greatest of early Christian missionaries, who, more than anyone—after Jesus—shaped Christian thinking and the form the fledgling communities would take, had a clear purpose in taking the road to the ancient city of Damascus, then a Roman province. Still a respected Jewish leader, single-mindedly set on persecuting Christians, armed with letters from the High Priest in Jerusalem for the synagogues in Damascus, he intended to bring any followers of "The Way"[3] he discovered there—both men and women—back to Jerusalem as prisoners, bound in ropes.

We will never know the full truth of what happened on this road. The Damascus event has become paradigmatic for all conversions. What the writer of the Acts of the Apostles describes so dramatically (Acts 9.1–22), Paul himself understood as an appearance of the Risen Christ (1 Corinthians 15.8–9). The crucial point for Christian faith has always been that this faithful, learned Jew underwent a total transformation. All Creation for him was bathed in a different light as his world view was transformed and he began to proclaim Jesus as the Son of God. Before leaving Damascus he was electrifying the astounded Jewish community there by proclaiming Jesus as the Christ. His conversion and subsequent passionate commitment to proclaiming the truth of Christ has blazed a trail for all who follow. Paul, according to his own account, then preached in Damascus before travelling south to Arabia for three years (Galatians 1.15–18).

There are, however, other even earlier traditions or legends associated with the growth of Christianity in Syria. One such tradition is reported by the fourth-century historian Eusebius of Caesarea, who relates how Abgar, King of Edessa, heard talk of Jesus and invited him to come and stay with him to escape the snares of the Jews. Jesus promised to send him one of his disciples, Addai (Thaddeus), who would proceed to evangelise Edessa.[4] The Christian community of Antioch was founded by those who fled Jerusalem after Stephen's martyrdom (Acts 11.19–21). Paul's fellow missionary, Barnabas, was delegated by the Church of Jerusalem to organise that community (Acts 11.25–26):

> Then Barnabas departed to Tarsus to seek Saul, and when he had found him, he brought him unto Antioch. And it came to pass that for a whole year they assembled themselves with the church, and taught a great many.[5]

The Book of Acts adds a very important clue for the future: "And the disciples were called Christians first in Antioch" (Acts 11.26). Paul was linked to the Church of Antioch, modern *Antakieh* (just over the Turkish border), from which he set out on his many journeys in Asia Minor and Greece, travelling to such places as Corinth, Philippi, and Ephesus. After these missionary journeys, he came back to Antioch as to his home base. In this light, we can see Antioch as another cradle of Christianity as well as Jerusalem. Antioch is where Paul was joined by his companion Luke, an educated physician, who, as is well known, went on to write the third Gospel and the book we call the Acts of the Apostles; he would also accompany Paul on his final journey to Rome. While in Antioch, Paul confronted Saint Peter over his weak attitude with regard to the Judaisers (Galatians 2.11–14). Peter, it is thought, stayed for quite a long time at Antioch and is considered its first bishop

The purpose of this chapter is neither to chronicle Paul's journeys in detail nor to analyse the complexities of the tragic civil war that continues relentlessly in modern Syria. Rather, this is an attempt to understand the inspiration of the Spirit for the early Christian communities as they grew and flourished, and how this Spirit is now with Syria's Christians, who are presently living in affliction and who now, given the scale of their ever-escalating suffering, represent the Arab world's broken heart.

Syria—living with affliction 1: the richness of its Christian history

And so I ask, who now are the Christians in Syria and what is the background to its story of affliction? Muslims form now about 90 per cent of the Syrian people, and the Christian population has dropped from 10 per cent to 5.25 per cent in the last few years due to emigration caused by the seemingly endless conflict. According to World Watch Monitor, almost a third of Syria's Christians have left the country since the start of the civil war: Syria's most senior Catholic leader, Gregorios III Laham, the Melkite Greek Catholic Patriarch, noted that more than 450,000 of Syria's estimated 1.75 million Christians have left.[6] However, he said he remained sure that Syria's Christian community would survive.[7]

There are three main branches of Syrian Christianity—Eastern Orthodox, Catholic, and Protestant. Alongside these familiar forms of Christian denominations are smaller groups, such as the Maronites (founded in the fourth century by St Maro and in full communion with the Roman Catholic Church), the Armenian Orthodox Church, and the Melkites (who come under the jurisdiction of the Patriarch of Antioch). Considering the small fraction that this community contributes to the population of the region, it is difficult to imagine a time when Christianity did flourish in this country, with its strong centres in Damascus, Aleppo, and Homs (formerly Emesa). Moreover, these early Christians, with their numerous saints, churches, monasteries, and strong faith traditions since the days of Paul have been, tragically, almost forgotten by western Christianity, and yet have given a vibrancy to Christianity scarcely conceivable or experienced elsewhere.

William Dalrymple describes some of this richness in his acclaimed book, *From the Holy Mountain*, where he journeys from Mount Athos in Greece through Anatolia, Syria, and Israel to the Nile, terminating at the Kharga Oasis in central Egypt, which is the southern frontier of Byzantium before the Arab conquests of the mid-seventh century.[8] He comments sadly on the disappearing Christians in the many countries he visits, and this was long before the current conflict. His words on Syria, written over a decade before the current conflict erupted, were prophetic (emphasis is mine):

> But if the pattern of Christian suffering was more complex than I could possibly have guessed at the beginning of this journey, it was also more desperate. In Turkey and Palestine, the extinction of the descendants of John Moschos's Byzantine Christians seemed imminent . . . Only in Syria had I seen the Christian population looking happy and confident, *and even their future seemed uncertain, with most expecting a backlash as soon as Assad's repressive minority regime began to crumble.*[9]

Yet even after the seventh-century Arab conquest, following the seeds sown by Paul, and the subsequent flourishing of the faith, Christians were still in the majority. With the conquest, Arabic became the main language. The Revd Nadim Nassar, a Syrian Anglican priest in Britain and Director of the Awareness Foundation in London, describes relations between Christians and Muslims before the present war as positive:

> Syria enjoyed decades of harmonious relationships between the minorities and the Sunni majority; people made friends and did business together regardless of religion or denomination. Unlike in the West, adherents of all religions

> belonged to the same culture and ethnic background; we shared a common language, as well as many traditions. For example, Muslims would come out of their homes to be part of our Christmas celebrations, and Christians would join Muslims in the Iftar (breaking the fast) in Ramadan.[10]

Still, Dalrymple had described the situation of Christians in the Levant as a small minority of 14 million "struggling to keep afloat amid 180 million non-Christians with their numbers shrinking annually through emigration."[11] This was 1997, and the numbers of Christians are still decreasing, as indeed they are in many countries of the Middle East. One of the tragedies of the present situation is that, as Dalrymple and others describe, Syria used to be a place to which other Christians (like the Iraqi Chaldeans) fled when they were under threat, *but now it is Syrian Christians themselves who flee.* As Dalrymple reported the Metropolitan of the Syrian Orthodox Church of Aleppo as saying:

> "Christians are better off in Syria than in anywhere else in the Middle East," said Mar Gregorios emphatically. "Other than Lebanon this is the only country in the region where a Christian can really feel the equal of a Muslim . . . In Syria there is no enmity between Christian and Muslim. If Syria were not here, we would be finished. Really. It is a place of sanctuary, a haven for all Christians.[12]

So how could Syrian Christianity have now reached this point of utter desolation? First, it is necessary to understand the political realities:

> The conflict in Syria will not end with the death of Assad or the removal of his regime. Not if the guns are put away and a new government is formed. It can only end when the atrocities of the war are lost from living memory, because they will not be forgiven.[13]

Such is the bleak—and recent—assessment by journalist Paul Danahar. The political strategist Emile Hokayem understands that Syria is at the intersection of profound political and strategic trends extending across the Middle East; the Arab world's crucial fault lines run through Syria and he identifies five key factors which contribute to instability in the region.[14] The first of these is the breakdown between government and society which has led to the Arab revolts. Secondly, the intensifying struggle over regional dominance between Iran and several Arab States, notably Saudi Arabia. The third is the growing Sunni-Shia rift, especially in Iraq and Lebanon, the repercussions of which are felt in Syria. The fourth is the rise of political Islam, and the incumbent implications for the identity of Arab States, and secular and non-Muslim groups within them, right across the Middle East. This final factor is the balance between ethnic groups whereby once marginalised minorities seek to express their identity. Jonathan Kuttab, a Palestinian lawyer, notes additional complexities, including the Kurdish/Arab antagonism and the Sunni/Sunni tension; as part of this latter struggle, Salafists are in conflict with those calling themselves "Takfiri", with one idea in mind: too kill their opponents.[15] Al-Qaida fits within this category. And it should not be forgotten that Qatar and Saudi Arabia are pouring money into the conflict.

So, how do the Christian communities fit within this analysis? It is frequently said that Christians are Alawites and are therefore connected with the regime of President Assad and his family. The reality is more complex:

The Alawite minority, from which the ruling clique hails, represents between 10 and 12 per cent of the 22 million strong Syrian population; the Christian communities, 10 per cent;[16] the mostly Sunni Kurdish community, around 10 per cent; the Sunni Arab majority, close to 65 per cent;[17] Ismaili, Druze, Shia and other minorities account for the remainder.[18]

The Assad regime, to counterbalance the Sunni majority, has reached out to Sunni and Christian merchant elites, "to lock them into a bargain that secured their fortunes in exchange for loyalties."[19] But, as Hokayem writes, it is important to distinguish Alawite relatives and associates of the Assad family from the majority community. He adds that it is difficult to understand, due to the limited research available, whether the Alawite community as a whole has benefitted from the Assad regime and its discriminatory policies.

In contrast, the Revd Stephen Griffith writes that the Assad regime was a violent regime from the beginning, and that the Sunni Muslims were specifically targeted, with the threat of rape being also used as a tool of subjugation.[20] Sometimes Christians clung too closely to the regime for protection, as Griffith wrote:

> When I visited a new Syrian Orthodox Bishop in 1996, he gave me a gold lapel badge: not of the Cross but of the president: he had been lured by the regime's power, money and connections.[21]

This should not be seen as typical. Griffith also realises that the ancient Church of Syria, the Antiochians, was far more likely to distance itself from the regime:

> On President Bashar's accession in 2000, Patriarch Hazim preached about the need for moderate changes—a brave thing to do—and in the early days of the revolution, many Christians joined in the demonstrations across the country seeking reform.[22]

Once the civil war had started, the regime began to show its true colours in the cruelty it meted out on its own citizens. It was the story of Homs (ancient Emesa) that changed the whole picture:

> Homs was where the wider world learned of the savage brutality of the Assad regime . . . Homs was where the world began its betrayal of the Syrian people.[23]

Syria's second most ancient Christian city, Aleppo, suffered terribly:

> That ancient city, which had been inhabited for millennia, was in parts reduced to rubble. There was no electricity; water was scarce and rubbish was piling up in the streets . . . Families were forced to sell their possessions for food and heating oil as the bitter winter set in. People stood for

> hours in bread queues . . . If Homs was where the opposition realised they were going to have to fight the war alone, then Aleppo was where they realised what fighting a war actually meant.[24]

The situation continues to steadily worsen since these words were written.

Syria—living with affliction 2: the extent of the suffering

As this is an ongoing, tragic story, only certain aspects can be highlighted here. We remain in ignorance at the time of writing (March 2014) as to the fate of two prominent kidnapped members of the clergy in the northern province of Aleppo: the Syrian Orthodox and Greek Orthodox bishops of Aleppo, Mor Yohanna Ibrahim and Boulos Yazigi.[25] Before the kidnapping, they had both constantly called for talks to end the crisis and had warned of the threat posed by the Syrian conflict to religious tolerance. They were seized by a terrorist group in the village of Kfar Dael as they were carrying out humanitarian work. A Syriac member of the opposition Syrian National Coalition, Abdulahad Steifo, said the men had been kidnapped on the road to Aleppo from the rebel-held Bab al Hawa crossing with Turkey.[26] This kidnapping awoke international attention to the gravity of the war. To this day it is not known if they are alive or dead. The Syrian Orthodox Church has been further weakened by the death of the Patriarch, Athanasius, on 21 March 2014.

The second issue that finally awoke international conscience and concern was more recent: the strategic and ethical question in relation to the use of chemical weapons. The alleged chemical weapons attack on Ghouta, just outside Damascus, happened on the 21 August 2013; over 3,600 people were hospitalised and at least 355 died.[27] But Syria's Christian leaders opposed plans by some countries in the West to increase the militarization of the region in response to the chemical attacks, claiming it would lead to more deaths and more misery for the country's civilians. Gregorios III, the Melkite Greek Catholic Patriarch of Antioch, told *Aid to the Church in Need* that "it is time to finish with these weapons and, instead of calling for violence, international powers need to work for peace."[28] Besides the Church, many other groups have spoken out against supplying weapons. Despite this, the United States began to provide armaments to opposition military groups in August 2013.[29]

The United Nations claims that, between the beginning of the conflict in the spring of 2011 and the middle of 2013, violence in Syria had claimed more than 100,000 lives.[30] With entire towns and villages empty and in ruins, at least four million people were displaced within the country, while two million others had fled across Syria's borders. At the time of publication (October 2013), the report of *Aid to the Church in Need* predicted that, by 2014, 10 million people—nearly half the country's pre-war population—would be in urgent need of aid, making it the worst disaster in the UN's history.[31] Religious persecution, the report continues, has played a crucial part in the conflict in Syria, which the UN's High Commissioner for Refugees called "the worst humanitarian crisis since the end of the Cold War." Christians have suffered greatly, as indeed have many communities. Islamist violence was mostly directed against other Muslims, but Christians were also very much at risk:

> Seen as sympathetic to President Assad's regime, Christians were victim to attacks from the rebel Free Syrian Army; on the other hand, seen as sympathetic to the West by virtue of their shared Christian faith, they were a target for forces loyal to the regime and fearful of international pressure mounting against the Syrian government. Such problems were compounded by the fact that Christians were most populous in regions where the violence was often most severe.[32]

Homs (home to Syria's second largest Christian community) showed the extent of the crisis being faced by the Christian community. Thousands upon thousands of Christians fled the city. In Homs' Christian quarter, eight or more ancient churches and other religious buildings were desecrated and ruined. Extremist soldiers also targeted mainstream Muslims. Christians fled Homs for the nearby Valley of the Christians, home to numerous Christian-majority towns and villages.

Emergency aid was urgently requested by leading charities amid reports that other organisations were ignoring the particularly severe crisis endured by Christians. Although persecution of Christians was not as prevalent as some reports suggested, for some it was very real. *Aid to the Church in Need* interviewed the Enser family who fled to Jordan from Damascus, where in early 2011 they encountered Islamists who stated: "Don't celebrate Easter otherwise you will be killed like your Christ".[33] Claims of an anti-Christian dimension to the conflict became irrefutable when it became clear that clergy were a particular risk. Some were targeted after seeking to negotiate with terrorists for the release of kidnapped Christians. The October 2012 abduction and brutal killing of Fr Fadi Haddad, the parish priest of Qatana caused widespread shock.

The killing and abduction of clergy, the desecration of churches, and ongoing violence and intimidation left many Christians with no option but to leave. Hence the massive decline already referred to: some displacement camps and refugee centres have reported a disproportionate number of Christians. By the summer of 2013, human rights observers were reporting that the "majority" of Iraqi Christians in Syria had fled.[34] The signs indicated that unless there was a dramatic change for the better, many, if not most, of Syria's indigenous Christians would do the same.[35] The Church in Syria, the survivor of severe persecution dating back almost to Christianity's beginnings with the mission of Paul, has clearly entered one of its most perilous periods.[36]

Nor can the West claim to be in ignorance of what is happening. In October 2012, the Catholic bishop of Aleppo, Antoine Audo, was in Britain, during which time he addressed a meeting in the Houses of Parliament of MPs, charity leaders and peers, the House of Lords, making an appeal for human rights and religious freedom. He said, "Aleppo, the city I love so much and where I have been bishop this past twenty years, is now devastated—much of it in ruins."[37] Mentioning that people of all faiths had suffered, he stressed the plight of Christians, stating that the exodus of faithful "would be a catastrophe," continuing to say:

> If we Christians in my country were reduced to a token few, it would be disastrous, because, until now, ours has been one of the last remaining strong Christian centres in the whole of the Middle East. And so I ask: what is the future of Christianity in the Middle East now?[38]

The refugee crisis in Syria is the worst that United Nations and United Nations Works and Relief Agency (UNWRA) have ever known. More than 2.5 million Syrians have fled their homes since the outbreak of civil war in March 2011, taking refuge in neighbouring countries or within Syria itself. According to the United Nations High Commissioner for Refugees (UNHCR), over 600,000 have fled to immediate neighbours Turkey, Lebanon, Jordan and Iraq.[39] Yet the real number of Syrians refugees in these countries is much higher, perhaps double UNHCR statistics, which only record those officially registered as refugees: "Syria is haemorrhaging women, children and men who cross borders often with little more than the clothes on their backs," said the UNHCR.[40] The increase of nearly 1.8 million people over the past twelve months is an 'alarming' trend, the agency said, warning that, so far, there is 'no sign of this tragic outflow ending'.[41]

Furthermore, what is very disturbing is that many of the refugees are escaping only to find themselves in a different sort of danger, as the following story tragically describes: Hayam, a 25-year-old mother of three in neighboring Lebanon's Beqaa Valley, said she and a friend visited a local organization that was distributing food and were told they needed to drive to a nearby warehouse. There, they encountered a group of men. "They attacked us. We started to scream and cry," the woman said, explaining the men attempted to rape them and asked, "Why are you scared? Nothing happened. You are married. Why are you afraid of this? It's not your first time." Hayam said she could not report the men. "They will kill me, or they will send me to my parents, and *they* will kill me. We are a tribal society," she said.[42]

Another refugee, 14-year-old Rahaf in Beirut, said she was cornered by teenagers while on her way to clean houses, which she has been doing for extra money. "They scared me. They made me hate life," the girl said.

Her mother said her daughter told her, "Mama, I would rather die in our country than have these problems."[43]

The number of affected people given by United Nations—more than 100,000—includes many civilians, since the popular uprising in Syria spiraled into a civil war in 2011. "Syria has become the great tragedy of this century—a disgraceful humanitarian calamity with suffering and displacement unparalleled in recent history," said Antonio Gutiérrez, the United Nations High Commissioner for refugees.[44] His statement strikes an even deeper note by the way all the aid agencies at work in the region—International Red Cross, Oxfam, Catholic Agency for Overseas Development (CAFOD), Christian Aid, Care International, Médecins sans Frontières, and Tear Fund—have all placed Syria on the highest level of priority in terms of both the war in general and their own work for refugees in particular—which is heroic.[45]

Another heartbreaking dimension should not be overlooked. The NGO *Save the Children* has highlighted the suffering of children as a crucially important dimension of the crisis. These children are being robbed of childhood. The story of a father who lives with his family in Za'atari refugee camp in Jordan illustrates this poignantly (emphasis is mine):

> My son was born in a shelter, under bombs. He is now seven months old.
>
> I remember the day he was born. The shelling started at 10 p.m. We were at home and there was no electricity because it had been bombed out. The bombs didn't stop, so we were forced to run to the shelter. My wife was on the brink of giving birth, and I knew we needed a doctor. We had no medicines. I left the shelter and ran to find a doctor. I found one who was helping injured people. He came back with me and together we helped my wife give birth safely.
>
> My only concern is for my children. They are the sole reason I decided leave.
>
> The bombardment was haphazard—there were absolutely no certain timings for it to take place. The shelling was unbearable, especially for our children. They were so scared. There was no way to say where the next shell would come

from. We are now familiar with bombardments. When the first shell fell, we would run to the shelter. We didn't wait to see how close it was, we didn't wait until our house was destroyed to run.

There was no water or electricity in the shelter—it was pitch black. The children were exhausted, thirsty and hungry. We tried to take food to the shelter but it ran out so quickly. Sometimes we stayed for three days in the shelter, and then we were forced to leave to get food and water—we risked the bullets and the shells to feed our family.

What am I most worried about? My children. What did they do to deserve this? What crime? The only way to keep them safe was to leave Syria. I have seen with my own eyes children's bodies in my town, dead and covered with sand. I feel as if every dead child was my own. We tried to save whoever we could and the rest we dug out from the rubble with our own hands.

World leaders have watched this now for over a year and a half. It is time for action. I feel as though Syria is fading away because of this inhumanity. *I feel as if every dead child was my own.*[46]

A snapshot of life in the refugee camps

"At a summer camp for hundreds of Syrian refugee children, the mission went well beyond the sports, painting, music, and storytelling that were part of the programme"; these are the words of Aziz Abu Sarah, who recently spent a few weeks at this camp along the Turkey-Syria border with his Syrian colleague Nousha Kabawat, the program officer for Syria at the Center for World Religions, Diplomacy, and Conflict Resolution at George Mason University, and six other volunteers who operated the summer camp.[47]

These were deeply traumatized children, says the report—some seventy-five of them were orphans. Many yearned for the kind of school learning that most children take for granted, but which is not generally available in refugee camps. Aziz Abu Sarah was heartbroken to witness bereavement and sometimes even the first expressions of radicalization and cynicism in these children. He makes several important points: first, that many refugees are not counted and that, consequently, the real number of refugees could be much higher. The United Nations officially estimates that there are more than two million Syrian refugees in neighboring countries. This number refers to refugees who registered with the United Nations upon leaving Syria and arriving in a refuge country. However, the author met many Syrians in Turkey and Jordan who have not registered as refugees and therefore are not included in the UN total. Secondly, the report shows how host countries are struggling to absorb the large numbers of refugees with their current infrastructure. In Lebanon, for example, a population of 4.2 million people is hosting 716,000 Syrian refugees. No country in the world has the ability to cope with a 17 per cent increase in its population over a mere twelve months. Jordan, which had a major problem with water before the arrival of Syrian refugees, found itself in a water crisis this past year. In May, when Aziz Abu Sarah visited Jordan's Za'atari camp—now home to 144,000 refugees—there were long lines to fill bottles of water, and Jordanians outside the camp complained continuously about their own lack of water.

A third challenge facing host countries is that many refugees do not live in camps. Some of these refugees live in poor conditions with less help from international organizations, but they prefer being free to being contained within fenced camps. Fourthly, there is a major problem adjusting to the needs of refugee children, who comprise more than half of the refugee population. Absorbing them in the current school system is impossible, but starting new schools has proved to be extremely difficult. As a result, many children have not attended school in the past two years. To frustrate matters further, the international community—already overwhelmed by the basic humanitarian needs of Syrian refugees—is in no position to adequately respond to the critical challenge of education: in the midst of an armed conflict and dire humanitarian need, education is seen as a secondary need. But, Aziz Abu Sarah warns, in five years' time, due to this lack of foresight, the world will have to deal with an uneducated, and very possibly disenfranchised, generation that is ripe for radicalization. More than four million Syrians are displaced within Syria. Furthermore, the living conditions in camps within Syria are much worse than in those in Turkey, Lebanon, or Jordan. Lack of food, medicine, and water is apparent. Unlike refugees in camps outside Syria, displaced Syrians—whether they are in camps or not—are within firing range and therefore always in danger. Many displaced people have been displaced multiple times in their search for safety. One of the worst elements is that refugee camps are like a prison:

> The moment you enter a refugee camp, you are registered and confined to a gated and fenced space that you are not allowed to exit and re-enter of your own free will. The camp is guarded by armed police officers who control your daily routine. Perhaps the worst thing about camps is that there is no way to be productive. Camps offer no work possibilities, and just like in prison, you receive your daily portion of food and water and are asked to wait, hopelessly, passively.[48]

Because of these conditions, some decide to return to Syria despite the danger.

Thus ends Aziz Abu Sarah's report: the future of Syria will not be decided only on the battlefield but also by millions of refugees and displaced people. Despite intense need in many other humanitarian areas, he calls on the international community must focus on education, health care, and trauma therapy so that these Syrians can contribute to a better future for their country when the armed conflict is over.

The content of Aziz Abu Sarah's report can be multiplied by the many accounts of people from a variety of NGOs. I will end here by citing a poignant description of a visit to a camp by Mariam Tadros, a trustee of the NGO *Embrace the Middle East* (emphasis is mine):

> One of the most draining days, emotionally and spiritually, was the day in Zahle, visiting Syrian Refugee families. We'd been faced with the immensely urgent crises every single

> day of the trip and this visit really was the climax of that. Stories of families torn apart, children with nothing to do, not enough food on the table, no income, living in tents or within 4x4 concrete walls. The need of every single family was so immense that all the work being done by all the agencies is only scratching the surface. We could tangibly feel the changing face of Lebanon and the tide shifting, it felt like it wasn't long before this crisis turned to disaster. The stories we heard from inside Syria, both from the families we met and from the report from the Pontifical Mission: homes destroyed, family members kidnapped, cities demolished—narrative that were and still are numbing.
>
> This summary doesn't do any justice to the sheer depth and power we felt with every single partner and project we visited. I'm reminded of words from a book I recently read that say: "This Kingdom is a lot more like a tree. God is looking for gardeners, not guards. A guard is trained in a defensive stance of fear and suspicion. A gardener is motivated by love and creativity." *All those that we met were gardeners, creators of hope and love for those they served.* In a country so in need of unity and grace, they all provide a glimpse of that, together breaking through the brokenness with light.[49]

Where is the Holy Spirit in Syria?

Mariam Tadros's words about encountering "gardeners of hope" inspire this search. I began this chapter with the optimism of Paul's conversion and the joy of the early communities as they grew and spread, despite opposition and, in many cases, persecution. This is the first link of those early Christians with today's embattled communities. Their experience of the presence of the Spirit is moulded by their lives of shared affliction.

This shared affliction is woven into the depths of Christian spiritual life. St Isaac the Syrian, a seventh-century hermit of the Assyrian Church of the East, wrote (emphasis is mine):

> The desire of the Spirit for those in whom the spirit dwells is not to let them grow accustomed to laziness, or to invite them to a life of ease, but rather to one of labours *and much affliction*. Accordingly the Spirit teaches them wakefulness, strengthens them in trials, and brings them to wisdom.[50]

This strength and perseverance is the amazing witness of Syrian Christians. How many times have I heard Christians being asked how they manage to endure in the midst of persecution only to hear the reply, "We follow the Lord."

The special gifts and fruits of the Holy Spirit are what enable these "gardeners of hope". Traditionally, these fruits are manifest in forbearance under suffering, patience, patient endurance (= *sumud*) and steadfastness under provocation, forbearance under ill-will, and the ability to endure persecution and ill-treatment.[51] And this persecution is a daily event. As I write (6 November 2013), the Syriac Orthodox Metropolitan of Homs and Hama, Archbishop Selwanos Boutros Alnemeh, has reported the worst massacre of Christians in Syria since the beginning of the country's internal conflict began in 2010 in the town of Sadad, north of Damascus. He decried the world's silence in the face of the atrocity. Islamist militias had invaded the Christian town of Sadad at the end of October 2013, only to be promptly re-conquered by the Syrian army. "Forty-five innocent civilians were martyred for no reason, and among them several women and children, many thrown into mass graves," reported Metropolitan Selwanos.[52] We cannot ignore his plea the world:

> We have cried out to the world for help but no one has listened to us. Where is the Christian conscience? Where is human consciousness? Where are my brothers? I think of all those who are suffering today in mourning and discomfort: We ask everyone to pray for us . . . There is a lump in the

> throat and burning in the heart for all that's happened in my metropolitanate and its poor suffering people.[53]

The grief of the Holy Spirit—an ancient Scriptural theme[54]—at such an atrocity and at the entire deteriorating situation in Syria must seize our attention. Even if Eastern and Western theology differ in their understanding of the theology and action of the Spirit, both hold fast to the centrality of Trinitarian faith, especially in times of affliction. Communion between God and the human being through the Spirit is at the heart of this:

> God's very self is poured forth through the Holy Spirit into the human being in such a way that the human subject is in partnership with God.[55]

The Russian orthodox theologian, Paul Evdokimov, citing St Basil, affirms that the human being does not possess any gift that goes not come from the Spirit. The Spirit reunites the human being with God, being the giver of life and treasury of grace.[56]

With this in mind, it can be said that the grieving Spirit of God shares the affliction of the Syrian people. This is not a new theme: what happened between Jesus and God on the Cross at Calvary was, at its heart, a Trinitarian event. What we observe is an afflicted Christ giving himself to the will and love of the Creator God. But what must also be true is that—as Moltmann and others have argued—this suffering and affliction enters the being of the Godhead.[57] Our God is a suffering God. And what was the role of the Spirit? Surely, it is to hold Father and Son together in an agony of suffering love and hope? As John Taylor, former Bishop of Winchester wrote:

> What was the Holy Spirit doing at Calvary? First, in a mystery we cannot plumb he must have been about his eternal employ between the Father and the Son, holding each in the awareness of each other in an agony of bliss and love that must forever lie infinitely beyond our understanding.

> For Jesus this involved the forsakenness and the ultimate trust.[58]

Will this suffering love and hope sustain Syrian Christians in this hour of desperation?

Notes

1. Mark Twain, *The Innocents Abroad* (1989), cited in Terry Carter, Lara Dunston, and Amelia Thomas, *Syria and Lebanon*, (London: Lonely Planet, 2008), p. 79.
2. To avoid confusion I refer to him consistently as Paul not Saul. See earlier note in Chapter 2.
3. This is how the early Christians named their calling. It was in Antioch that they were first called Christians.
4. Ignace Dick, "Christian Syria", in *Living Stones Year Book 2013: Christianity in the Middle East: Theology, History, Politics, and Dialogue* (London: Melisende, 2013), p. 71.
5. RSV has "A large company of people".
6. "One third of Syrian Christians have gone, says cleric", World Watch Monitor (23 October 2013), <https://www.worldwatchmonitor.org/2013/10/2763901/>.
7. Ibid.
8. William Dalrymple, *From the Holy Mountain: A Journey in the Shadow of Byzantium*, (London; Harper-Collins, 1997). Reprinted by permission of HarperCollins Publishers Ltd. © William Dalrymple 1997.
9. Ibid., p. 448. John Moschos was a sixth century monk. Dalrymple retraces Moschos' own journey as described in his book, *The Spiritual Meadow*, John Wortley (trans) (Kalamazoo; Cistercian Publications, 1992).
10. Nadim Nassar, "Weapons Don't Stop War", in *The Tablet* (22 June 2013), p. 6. Reproduced with permission of the publisher; <http://www.thetablet.co.uk>.
11. Dalrymple, *From the Holy Mountain*, p. 19.
12. Ibid., p. 150.

13. Paul Danahar, *The New Middle East: the World After the Arab Spring* (London: Bloomsbury, 2013), p. 372. © Paul Danahar, 2013.
14. Emile Hokayem, *Syria's Uprising and the Fracturing of the Levant* (Abingdon: Routledge, 2013), p. 10.
15. Jonathan Kuttab, workshop in Sabeel Conference, Jerusalem (November 2013).
16. As written above, this has dropped to 5.25%.
17. Other sources say 73%: Hokayem, discusses this disputed figure in *Syria's Uprising*, p. 20, footnote 3.
18. Hokayem, *Syria's Uprising*, p. 17.
19. Ibid., p. 19.
20. Stephen Griffith, "Nostalgia for the regime of Assad", in *The Church Times* (25 October 2013), p. 15. The Revd Stephen Griffiths was the Anglican Chaplain in Syria before the war began, from 1997 to 2003. Bashar-al-Assad's father took power in 1970, his son in 2000.
21. Ibid.
22. Ibid.
23. Danahar, *The New Middle East*, p. 380.
24. Ibid., p. 404.
25. Reported by Mathew Weaver, "Syria crisis: Aleppo bishops kidnapped", *The Guardian* (23 April 2014).
26. Some sources say they are still alive. According to Turkey's Foreign Ministry, which says it is continuing to petition for their release: "Our efforts to rescue them are still under way," said a statement. "We are doing our best to ensure anyone who has been kidnapped in Syria is saved, as our minister had previously expressed. Men of religion have an added significance. Turkey is making every effort so the metropolitans can be saved. Although we are not 100 per cent certain, we have reason to believe they are alive." I have no means of verifying this.
27. This is according to the recent report of Aid to the Church in Need, *Persecuted and Forgotten: A Report on Christians Oppressed by their Faith* (October 2013), p. 142.
28. Ibid.
29. Ibid.
30. Ibid.
31. Ibid., p. 141.

32. Ibid.
33. Ibid., p. 143.
34. Ibid.
35. Ibid., p. 144.
36. The report chronicles in detail numerous atrocities, murders, and mutilations committed against people and churches in Syria's Christian centres. In April 2013, the Melkite Greek Catholic Patriarch Gregorios III of Antioch detailed atrocities against Christians since the conflict began in early 2011. He said 1,000 Christians had been killed, that "entire villages have been cleared of their Christian inhabitants," and that more than 40 churches and other religious buildings had been damaged or destroyed. In a desperate appeal for dialogue, he said, "The whole of Syria has become a battlefield . . . Every aspect of democracy, human rights, freedom, secularism and citizenship is lost from view and no-one cares"; ibid., pp. 141–147.
37. Mark Greaves, "The City I love is in ruins", *The Catholic Herald* (18 October, 2012).
38. Ibid.
39. Jethro Mullen, "Number of Syrian refugees rises above 2 million, U.N. agency says", (4 September 2014), <http://edition.cnn.com/2013/09/03/world/meast/syria-refugees-unhcr/>. The following quotations are taken from this article.
40. Ibid.
41. Ibid.
42. Ibid.
43. Ibid.
44. "Two million Syrians are refugees", UNHCR Press Release (3 Spetember 2013), <http://www.unhcr.org/522484fc9.html>.
45. Another issue here is the great difficulty of maintaining impartiality in giving aid. Simon Jenkins describes convoys being turned back at checkpoints because they were considered to be helping the wrong side! See Simon Jenkins, "The Red Cross needs to Reclaim its hi-jacked Neutrality", in *The Guardian* (1 November 2013).
46. *Untold Atrocities: the Story of Syria's Children* (London: Save the Children, 2012), p. 21.

47. Aziz Abu Sarah is an executive director at the Center for World Religions, Diplomacy, and Conflict Resolution at George Mason University in Fairfax, Virginia, and a National Geographic Emerging Explorer for 2011. Much of this section is a summary of Aziz Abu Sarah, "First person: five things I learned in Syrian refugee camps", *National Geographic* (September 2013), <http://news.nationalgeographic.com/news/2013/09/130920-syria-refugees-camps-war-children/>. This was his third visit to the camps in Syria, Turkey, and Jordan.
48. Ibid.
49. This is a shortened version of Mariam Tadros, "Lebanon", from her blog *Nomad Heart* (24 April 2013) . The book Tadros refers to is Shane Hipps: *Selling Water by the River* (Faith Words, 2012).
50. Sebastian Brock (ed. and trans.), *The Wisdom of Saint Isaac the Syrian*, (Oxford: SLG Press, 1997), Homily 60, B 423, p. 10.
51. Mike Bradley, "Long Suffering—The 4th Fruit of the Holy Spirit", *Ezine Articles* (20 January, 2008), <http://www.ezinearticles.com/?id=938887>.
52. "Orthodox Bishop Decries Largest Massacre of Syrian Christians", *Zenit* (5 November 2013), <http://www.zenit.org/en/articles/Orthodox-Bishop-Decries-Largest-Massacre-of-Syrian-Christians>.
53. Ibid.
54. "And do not grieve the Holy Spirit", Ephesians, 4.30.
55. Sylvie Avakian, "The Mystery of Divine Love in the Apophatic Theology of Bishop George Khodr", in *Theological Review*, 33 (2012), pp. 39–68, quotation p. 46.
56. Paul Evdokimov, *L'Orthodoxie*, (Paris: Desclée de Brouwer, 1965), p. 111; my paraphrase and translation.
57. Jürgen Moltmann, *The Suffering God* (London: SCM, 1974); and John V. Taylor, *The Go-Between God* (London: Collins, 1972).
58. Taylor, *The Go-between God*, p. 102.

CHAPTER 4

Out of Egypt have I called my son

> Everything in this country derives meaning from the River Nile: outside the Nile is death, as water brings life. The Nile is the supreme symbol of life, and the House of Life—opening up to all—and is Egypt's very dynamism.
>
> ***Bishop Thomas, Upper Egypt***[1]

> Open your hearts and your homes tonight,
> Welcome the dawn of hope;
> Throw wide the arms of your love today,
> Embrace the dawn of love.
>
> ***Kate McIhagga,*** **Into Egypt**[2]

A personal story: Coptic Easter celebrations in Upper Egypt

My search for the revelation of the Spirit in the lives of Christians—early and contemporary—led me to a country whose Christian roots go back to ancient times and whose history is intrinsically linked with Jewish and Christian heritage. "Out of Egypt have I called my son" wrote the prophet Hosea, and this clearly inspired the evangelist Matthew in his story of the Flight into Egypt of the Holy Family.[3]

Egypt is also, numerically, the most Christian country of the Middle East: there were about six to eleven million Christians before the current emigration, and they represent 10–12 per cent of the population.[4] The Copts are one of the oldest Christian communities in the Middle East.

Although integrated within the larger Egyptian nation, the Copts have survived as a distinct religious community, forming roughly 90 per cent of the Christian population, though estimates of course continue to vary. Modern Coptic Christians proudly trace their ancestry through an unbroken chain of patriarchs to the founding of their Church by St Mark, the evangelist and companion of St Peter, and their Church may have even earlier roots, as I would discover.[5] The Coptic Orthodox Church is headed by the Pope of Alexandria and the Patriarch of All Africa from the Holy See of Saint Mark, a position currently held by Pope Theodoros II.

I had two main reasons for going to Cairo at the beginning of May 2013. As we in the West were preparing for the Feast of the Holy Spirit at Pentecost, the Orthodox Church across the world was preparing to celebrate Easter with great solemnity—Easter Sunday in the Coptic Church would be on 5 May. Yet I knew from the theology of the Gospel of John that Easter was also the time when the Risen Jesus gave the Spirit to his apostles (John 20.22). My first reason was, consequently, how was the gift of the Holy Spirit being experienced by Coptic Christians in this time of affliction?

My second reason was the concern shared by many Christians in the West about the worsening sufferings of Christians in the Middle East. I knew that Christians had already been victims of recent violent incidents—two of them in the Coptic Cathedral of St Mark in Cairo itself. What I came to realise later was that, extraordinarily, my visit occurred at the time of an interlude between two revolutions, and it would be after the second that a period of greater danger would emerge for Christians.

Journey to Quosia, Upper Egypt, and the Good Friday Coptic experience

From this sense of wanting to be in solidarity, I flew to Cairo Airport to celebrate Easter with Coptic Christian communities. I began by looking at old Coptic Cairo. In all the churches I visited, Holy Week prayer was taking place, lasting about three hours each day. The churches themselves and the amazing Coptic Museum were witness to a deep-seated faith that has lasted for many centuries. But the most memorable experience was with the community of the Coptic Bishop Thomas in the diocese of Upper Egypt, in Quosia, a small town on the banks of the Nile, six hours journey by train south from Cairo.[6]

What was deeply impressive, and scarcely believable from a western Christian perspective, was that the whole community—including many small children—was present in church on Good Friday from 8.30 a.m. until 6 p.m. In fact, the church was packed with around a thousand people. It was almost unbearably hot, despite a few electric fans. And the whole community was fasting—this fast also meant not drinking water! Bishop Thomas explained the theological background to this to me: it implied a link with Creation before the fall, to the innocent time, the early relationship with God. "We were all created in the image of God—Genesis 1.26–27", he said, "and even though we lost the likeness through the Fall, we never lost the image". Fasting during Lent is an attempt to renew this relationship within the theology of Creation.

The idea of the Good Friday service from the Coptic tradition was to accompany Jesus hour by hour, from his arrest until he was dead and finally buried. The climax of the service was to chant a "*kyrie eleison*" (Lord have mercy) one hundred times facing north, then south, east, and west—four hundred times in all! Then the Bishop, along with his priests and deacons, processed around the Church with an icon of Jesus, which was then wrapped up with flowers and herbs and placed reverently on the altar. This represented the "burial" of the Lord.

After a short interval in which people were at last able to go home and eat, they were back in Church at 10 p.m.—for the whole night! This was the transition to the "Bright Saturday"—watching and waiting with the holy women as the Gospels relate, until the hour of Resurrection. The climax of the whole liturgy was the Mass of Easter, from midnight to 4 a.m., from Holy Saturday to Easter Sunday. Then the feasting began: the Lenten fast—which had meant refraining from milk and dairy products, meat and fish for more than forty days—was at last over.

Bishop Thomas and the current troubled situation

Bishop Thomas was generous with his time and very patient with my questions. When asked about the current difficulties faced by Coptic Christians, he said we must understand the issue within Egypt's history. Everything in this country derives meaning from the River Nile: outside the Nile is death, as water brings life. The Nile is the supreme symbol of life, the House of Life which is opened up to all; it is the source of Egypt's very dynamism. After the time of Alexander the Great (fourth century BC), the Ptolemaic dynasty created Alexandria to be a cosmopolitan city with no concept of military power. Similarly, when Christianity was founded, no concept of military power was involved (Christ offered an alternative source of power based on faith in the justice of God and the coming reign of God).

But with the coming of Islam in AD 640 two things happened. Firstly, the theological: the central tenet of Islam is that "There is one God, Allah, and Mohammed is his prophet" which was, according to Bishop Thomas, a direct attack on Christ, as Divine Son of God and with Islam came military power. Secondly, the sociological: as a result of the new power structures in Egypt, three groups arose. The first group, the new wave of Muslim conquerors, saw Egypt as a greener, nicer, fertile territory, and began to "marry" Egyptian women and then moved certain tribes to Egypt. They wanted to implement their belief that Islam and Arabic were superior. The second group consisted of Egyptian Christians who converted to Islam—their eyes were fixed on Arabia. This created a new atmosphere. Nonetheless, they still carried Egyptian culture with them. The third group were the Egyptians who remained Christian and became known as "Copts". There were now two cultural spheres in Egypt: Greco-Roman and Arab. Arabic became the dominant language. A very conversion-focused group wanted to apply Arabism everywhere, and to make a link with the Arabic empire. In spite of this, many Christians paid the *jizya* (tax) to the reigning powers, and continued to practise their faith in different, and often hidden, ways.

So now the question becomes: how did Egyptians deal with these issues in the past and how do they deal with them now? Since 1952, Egyptians have been free to leave the country: there are, for example, one million

Copts in the USA, and 400,000 in Canada. Coptic Christians have even gone to Georgia. This is the "Silent Exodus", and the Bishop finds the situation painful, but understands why people leave. The positive side of the emigration is that, in the diaspora, Coptic Christians create strong communities, help churches in Egypt financially, and create awareness of the situation and the struggles of Coptic Christians. Perhaps it as a result of the growing difficulties in Egypt, the disappointment with the consequences of the Revolution, the growing Islamization of the country, and the increasing poverty that now, in this context, Christians in Egypt find an identity and comfort within the churches, as they also do in the diaspora. The Bishop himself feels very strongly the responsibility which he has undertaken to create a "culture of excellence", and so he has founded a school in Quosia with a strong reputation and the intention of creating good leaders who will communicate with the whole society and strengthen people to stay in their homeland. In addition, at the new monastery of Anafora, which lies one hour's journey outside Cairo, he is building an inspirational community which is attracting many young people not only to the prayer and religious services but to stimulating educational programmes.

Figure 2: Anafora Monastery, outside Cairo

Figure 3: St John the Baptist Church at Quosia Upper Egypt, Good Friday.

The Bishop goes further: he has a vision of transformation for Church and society on three levels, or three directions of this transformation. First, he wants a movement from hierarchy to democracy, such that there would be a space to express ideas and feelings freely. Second, he wants to move from a male-dominated "pit of darkness" to a gender-equal society, using the teaching of the Bible to achieve this. He wants both women and men to be proud of their gender, and to be free to move forward together to greater understanding and sharing. Finally, he wants to move from a rigid religious orientation to a civil, spiritual, and open Egyptian society inclusive of all citizens. Anafora Monastery is the place where he tries to realise this transformation, to offer education on different levels and to build great leaders for Church and society. Bishop Thomas speaks with great enthusiasm. I saw his vision already being embodied in Quosia—in the guest house which is open and welcoming—as well as in Anafora, the newly burgeoning monastic community, but also in his hospitality and his willingness to give time for conversation at the busiest time of the Coptic year—Easter. I felt that, for the first time amidst the suffering and affliction of Arab Christians, that here the Spirit was at work not only with the gifts of courage and perseverance, but in leading communities into unknown areas of new forms of Christian community.

The ancient roots of Coptic faith

How did this deep-rooted faith emerge and retain its strength? The accepted story as advocated by the Coptic Church—which is a later tradition than that found in the Acts of the Apostles—is that in AD 49, about nineteen years after the Ascension of Jesus, St Mark travelled to Alexandria and founded the Church of Alexandria, which today is part of the Coptic Orthodox Church.[7] Aspects of contemporary Coptic liturgy can be traced back to Mark himself. He became the first bishop of Alexandria, and he is honored as the founder of Christianity in Africa.[8] This later tradition representing St Mark as the founder of the Church of Alexandria is mentioned by the historian Eusebius, St Jerome, the Apostolic Constitutions, Epiphanius, and many later authorities.[9] The date at which Mark came to Alexandria is still uncertain. It seems likely to have been during the reign of the Emperor Claudius (AD 41–4). Since Mark's successor was raised to episcopal status during the reign of Nero (probably about AD 61–2), Mark could have been Bishop of Alexandria for about twenty years.[10] What is vital for this story and this chapter is that, having followed Philip to Gaza and Paul to Damascus, that we now follow Mark (one of the seventy disciples, a companion of Peter and writer of the earliest Gospel, possibly coming from Cyrene in modern-day Libya) to Alexandria, known as the cradle of Egyptian Christianity. The Church of Alexandria is also the oldest Christian Church in Africa.[11]

This new foundation of Christianity had come directly from Palestine, but it now encountered a culture with other traditions. As Bishop Thomas told me, here everything begins from the Nile as bringing water, the gift of life. The story is told of the Egyptologist Margaret Murray who, in a mid-September night in a Coptic village in 1934, celebrated the night of the high Nile, giving thanks to the ruler of the river, no longer Osiris, the Egyptian god of the afterlife and resurrection in pre-Christian times, but Christ; she prayed for a blessing on the children of Egypt and their homes.[12] Indeed we know that the Coptic Church absorbed many influences from Pharaonic times, including the physical structure of churches and the development of liturgies from ancient rites. It is even said that the cult of Mary, the Mother of Jesus, developed from the great Egyptian Mother Goddess, Isis and her son Horus. It is little wonder that Egyptian Christians still love the many legends of the Holy Family's flight into Egypt through the Sinai Desert and the miracles associated with the Child Jesus,[13] an affection attested by many churches and shrines. Both modern and mediaeval historians concur that St Joseph received the vision from an angel at the Monastery Deir-el-Muharraq, telling him that it was safe to return to Palestine because those who wanted to kill the child had died. These sources are explicit about the time the Holy Family spent in Egypt—185 days, or over six months.[14]

The community which Mark founded made generously rich and enduring contributions to Christianity. The first was the Catechetical Tradition: the Catechetical School of Alexandria was the oldest catechetical school in the world. It was founded around AD 190 by the scholar Pantanaeus and became a famous institution of religious learning. Students were taught by such well-known scholars as Athenagoras, Clement, Didymus, and Origen, the last being an important, if controversial, theologian, especially in the field of commentary and comparative Biblical studies. But the scope of the Alexandrian school was not limited to theological subjects since science, mathematics, and humanities were also taught there. The famous question-and-answer method of commentary began at this Alexandrian School, and fifteen centuries before Braille, wood-carving techniques were in use there by blind scholars to read and write.

The second major contribution made by the Egyptians to Christianity was the creation, development, and organization of monasticism. Globally speaking, Christian monasticism stems, either directly or indirectly, from the Egyptian example. The most prominent figures of the monastic movement were Anthony the Great, Paul of Thebes, Macarius the Great, Shenouda the Archimandrite, and Pachomius the Cenobite. By the end of the fifth century, there were hundreds of monasteries, and thousands of cells and caves, scattered throughout the Egyptian desert. These sites have continued to attract pilgrims over the centuries who hoped to emulate the spiritual, disciplined lives of the Desert Fathers. Saint Basil the Great, Archbishop of Caesarea Mazaca and the founder and organiser of the monastic movement in Asia Minor, visited Egypt around AD 357 and his monastic rules are followed by the Eastern Orthodox Churches. Saint Jerome, who translated the Bible into Latin, came to Egypt while en route to Jerusalem around AD 400 and left details of his experiences in his letters. Among the many visitors to the desert monks was a young man called John Cassian. On his return to Europe he founded a monastic community for women and men in Marseilles around the year 415; by the end of that century, the ideas of desert monasticism would reach as far as Ireland. Cassian responded to the request of a local bishop to compose a methodical presentation of the wisdom of the Desert Fathers. The result was his great work, *The Conferences of the Fathers*. Saint Benedict founded the Benedictine Order in the sixth century on the model of Saint Pachomius, although in a stricter form. Benedict recommended in his rule that the *Conferences* of Cassian should be read every day at mealtimes.[15] Such is the enduring influence of eastern monasticism on the West.

The third contribution of early Egyptian Christianity and the See of Alexandria's development of theology is their influence on the Church's Ecumenical Councils. The first three Ecumenical councils in the history of Christianity were led by Egyptian patriarchs. The Council of Nicaea (AD 325) was presided over by St Alexander, Patriarch of Alexandria, along with Saint Hosius of Córdoba. In addition, the most prominent figure of the council was the future Patriarch of Alexandria, Athanasius, who played the major role in the formulation of the Nicene Creed—which is still recited today in most Christian Churches across different denominations. One of the Council's decisions was to entrust the Patriarch of Alexandria with calculating and annually announcing the exact date of Easter to the rest of the Christian churches. The Council of Constantinople (AD 381) was presided over by Patriarch Timothy of Alexandria, while the Council of Ephesus (AD 431) was presided over by Cyril of Alexandria.

The situation of Coptic Christians today

First, we need to understand this in the context of two revolutionary events. On 25 January 2011, Egyptian people—notably young people—came together in Tahrir Square in Cairo, and in a coherently non-violent protest reclaimed a voice, an authority, and a power and managed to overthrow the government of President Mubarak. This experience was paradigmatic not only for Egyptians but for the protesting groups in other Middle Eastern countries. This is how Ahdaf Soueif encapsulates this historic moment in her Epilogue of *Cairo, My City, Our Revolution:*

> And I'll imagine you're reading this page here, in Cairo; the capital that's come back to her people, that's regained control of her land, her resources and her destiny; an Egypt that is part of a world that is on its way to finding a better, more equitable, more sustainable way of life for its citizens, where peoples' dreams and ambitions and inventiveness and imagination find an open horizon, and where variety and difference are recognized as assets in confident, vibrant, outward-looking communities.[16]

But it was not to be so simple. Euphoria soon vanished; I had picked this up this sense from many contacts during my own visit in May 2013. The new President, Mohammad Morsi (elected in summer 2012), disappointed all hopes. Young people gathered once more in Tahrir Square. On Tuesday, 23 July 2013, *The Guardian* reported that:

> A polarised Egypt is facing the most critical phase of its post-revolutionary life after Egypt's army ousted the country's elected president, Mohamed Morsi, and scheduled fresh elections in what was labelled by the presidency as a "full coup".[17]

The chief of the armed forces, General Abdel-Fatah al-Sisi, announced that he had suspended the constitution and would nominate the head of the constitutional court, Adli Mansour, as interim president that

Thursday.[18] Both presidential and parliamentary elections would follow shortly afterwards and a transitional cabinet would be named. After Morsi was officially deposed from office at 7 p.m., a statement appeared on the former president's Twitter and Facebook accounts which labelled the military move a "full coup". Late on the Wednesday night, a Muslim Brotherhood spokesman said Morsi was being held by the authorities in an unknown location. What followed, tragically, was a scenario of violence sharply contrasting with the earlier non-violent protest that had raised so many hopes:

> A security official said the head of the Muslim Brotherhood's political party and the Brotherhood's deputy chief had been arrested. State media said authorities had issued arrest warrants for 300 other Brotherhood members. At least 14 people were killed when Morsi opponents and supporters clashed after the army's announcement, state media and officials said . . . Three people were killed and at least 50 wounded in Alexandria . . . A further three died in the southern city of Minya . . . [19]

General Sisi strove to paint the coup as the fulfilment of the popular will, following days of vast protests against the former president Morsi's rule. "We will build an Egyptian society that is strong and stable, that will not exclude any one of its sons," he said.[20] He spoke of his "historic responsibility" in front of a panel of Egyptians representing what was intended to be full spectrum of Egyptian life, including the Coptic pope, the country's most senior Muslim cleric, and leading secular politician Mohamed El Baradei. His statement was met with rapturous applause—although five miles away in east Cairo, the mood could not have been more different. Here a rally of Morsi supporters booed Sisi's speech, chanting "Down with military rule", in scenes that epitomized Egypt's divisions. While secular Egyptians blame Morsi for autocratic policies that have failed to build consensus, Islamists are furious that Egypt's first democratically elected president should have been deposed after just a year in office.

While many on the street saw Morsi's removal as the continuation of Egypt's 2011 revolution, the ex-president's Islamist allies viewed it as a coup and a betrayal of democracy. And this ambivalence is echoed in international reactions:

> A democratically elected President had been violently removed. Thousands of Morsi supporters gathered in the streets to back him, many fearing that his departure would mark a return to the repressive treatment of Islamists under Mubarak. But, if Islamists saw Morsi's removal as a betrayal of democracy, for many in Tahrir it was a victory for people-power. US President Barack Obama reflected this anxiety in urging Egypt's armed forces to hand back control without delay to a democratic, civilian government. In a carefully worded statement, Obama said he was "deeply concerned" by the military's move to topple Morsi's government and suspend Egypt's constitution. He said he was ordering the US government to assess what the military's actions meant for US foreign aid to Egypt—currently $1.5bn a year in military and economic assistance.[21]

After this, the violence escalated: a day after Egypt's military-backed government declared the Muslim Brotherhood a terrorist group, a more aggressive crackdown was already emerging, as the authorities announced dozens of arrests across the country, followed by the seizure of land, stocks, and vehicles belonging to the Islamist movement's members. And so it went on with new levels of disruption: social and charitable groups even loosely associated with the Brotherhood struggled after their funds were frozen by the state. Egypt's new leaders clearly signalled that they had opened a wide-ranging and possibly protracted war on every facet of the Brotherhood's activities, with the "terrorism" designation giving the security forces greater latitude to stamp out a group deeply rooted in Egyptian social and civic life. The government had also sought to deny the group foreign help or shelter, urging other Arab governments to honour an antiterrorism agreement and shun the organization.

One of the operations caught in this violence was the Islamic Medical Association, a network of hospitals founded by a Brotherhood leader in the 1970s that now serves more than two million patients a year, mostly in poor neighbourhoods. A doctor at one of these facilities, Central Hospital in the Nasr City district of Cairo, said that, by the Thursday following Morsai's removal from office, admissions had already dropped by nearly half, with many apparently scared away by news that funding had been cut and worried that even going to the hospital would be seen by the security forces as supporting the Brotherhood. An administrator there said the hospital began turning away new patients. At another clinic in an impoverished corner of the Shubra neighbourhood, neonatal incubators were shut down to save on power expenses.

And so, *The Guardian* concluded:

> The reality—of a movement whose members are deeply integrated into Egypt's economic and social life, and a political force that has emerged after the uprising in 2011 as the most successful competitor in democratic elections—has muddied the government's portrait of the group and stymied a campaign to eradicate it after driving it from power in July.[22]

Coptic Christians after the second revolution

Christian communities in Egypt are witnessing a threat to their faith of increasing severity, with fears that the newly approved constitution fails to protect the rights of Christians.[23] Islamic groups continue to attack Christian buildings with little action by the police or security forces. On 16 January 2014, the Assyrian International News Agency reported that hundreds of Muslims destroyed a social services building belonging to the Coptic Church while chanting Islamic slogans.[24] Earlier the same month, a mob attacked Cairo's St Mark's Coptic cathedral, throwing rocks and fire bombs: "The police are not trying to protect us or do anything to stop the violence," said Wael Eskandar, a Coptic Christian activist, "On the contrary, they are actively aiding the people in civilian clothes in attacking Christians."[25] This attack followed several days of conflict, which included a gunfight in which four Christians and one Muslim died.[26] The Coptic Pope Tawadros II—who had recently succeeded the much loved Pope Shenouda III[27]—accused President Mohammed Morsi of failing to protect the cathedral in what was said to have been "an unprecedented direct criticism."[28] Tensions continued, with the Al Jazeera news agency reporting on 21 April that ten people had died in recent weeks during the clashes between Muslims and Coptic Christians in Egypt.[29]

It would get worse. Christians had quickly begun to despair of the regime that swept to power in the historic elections of 2012. Soon after becoming President, Mohammed Morsi set about creating a constitution which turned out to be explicit in its deference to Islamic sharia law.[30] In April 2012, the Coptic Orthodox Church announced its withdrawal from a panel charged with drafting Egypt's new constitution. Church representatives said it was "pointless" to continue participating on the panel saying Christians were unable to exert any influence.[31] The move prompted concerns that the new constitution would end up being written entirely by Islamist parties without due consideration of minority groups

Even before the constitution became law, the new Coptic Orthodox Patriarch Tawadros II spoke out against it, saying that a document "that hints at imposing a religious state must be absolutely rejected";[32] Coptic Catholic Bishop Kyrillos William agreed. Barely ten days after the constitution became law in December 2012, Bishop William told Aid to the Church in Need (ACN) that it "paved the way for an Islamic caliphate".[33] A week before the vote on the new constitution, 50,000 Islamists marched through the city of Assiut chanting that Egypt would be "Islamic, Islamic despite the Christians".[34] Men on horses rode around wielding swords in Christian districts of the city, evoking images of Muslims conquering Christians in the early years of Islam. According to local reports, Christians who tried to vote in some villages were pelted with stones and were forced to turn back before reaching the ballot box.[35]

In January 2013, Bishop William, acting administrator of the Coptic Catholic Church, was among three bishops who spoke out against the new constitution ratified by President Mohammed Morsi on 26 December

2012. Bishop William said: "We can see that the religious orientation of this constitution prepares the way for an Islamic caliphate."[36] The bishops—including Bishop Joannes Zakaria of Luxor and Bishop Antonio Aziz Minna of Giza—said the document explicitly upheld the pre-eminence of sharia in diverse aspects of law and government, and, in effect, took away key human rights of non-Muslims, women, and children.

Yet a note of hope has recently been expressed by Bishop Mouneer Anis, the Anglican Bishop of Egypt. On 25 October 2013, he said that Egypt's new constitution will accommodate non-Muslims and it is likely that its next government will not be Islamist.[37] Bishop Mouneer Anis, whose diocese also covers North Africa and the Horn of Africa, said that when a constitution was being drawn up following the ousting of President Hosni Mubarak, 70 per cent of the committee was Islamist, and, in the end, Christian representatives withdrew from the process.[38] That constitution, which was approved by President Mohamed Morsi in December 2013, drew on the principles of sharia law (as noted above). With the redrawing of the constitution under the new military regime, Bishop Anis has also said that this time the Christian representatives—Coptic and Catholic—have not withdrawn from the drafting process. He said that among the population there was less of an appetite for another Islamist government and a greater suspicion of Islamist politicians. Bishop Anis also regretted the US's decision, announced earlier in August 2014 to suspend a large part of the aid—including military equipment—that it sends to Egypt. He said it was a "superficial reading" to see Morsi as a democratically elected leader removed in a coup, going so far as to state that Morsi's "government was dictatorial and fascist."

Bishop Anis is one of many in Egypt who have questioned the validity of the election that swept Morsi to power, and he pointed out that the army immediately installed as interim president a top judge, namely chief justice Adly Mansour. When he was asked about Coptic Pope Tawadros's welcoming of the ousting of Morsi on Egyptian television, after which Morsi supporters attacked 139 churches and church buildings, the bishop said that the Coptic leader was merely expressing the "heart of all Egyptians", millions of whom had taken to the streets. He said he believes Islamists would have targeted the churches even if Tawadros had not spoken out.

Yet, despite this optimistic opinion, it cannot be denied that what has ensued between 2011 and 2013 was an unrelenting attack on Christian churches, related buildings, and individuals.[39] President Morsi's fall from office in July 2013 and Egypt's return to "temporary" military rule left many, if not most, people unable to predict what might follow:

> Would future historians look back at this point as the moment when the Islamist movement lost its influence as a force for change? Or was it no more than a temporary blip, with momentum still building towards a final show-down with pro-democracy campaigners. Either way, the stakes were high, and the future of Christianity in the region hung in the balance.[40]

As it still does. Yet, as this book nears completion, a calmer situation is evolving, despite levels of poverty on the increase. Egypt looks to the next presidential elections, hoping for a candidate who will be capable of holding all opposing factions together and offering a realistic chance of a society in peace.

Where is the Holy Spirit?

When I asked this question at the end of Chapter 3, in the context of the affliction of Syrian Christians, I suggested that the affliction of the people was brought into the heart of the Trinitarian love between Father and Son; that our God is a suffering God who shared this affliction. But there are ever-deepening dimensions to this story: God does far more than suffering with God's people—otherwise, from where would hope spring? If I can use the analogy of a mother's love for her sick child: a mother feels compassionate suffering love when a child is very sick. She often wishes she could take the pain and suffer it herself instead of her child. But suffering is not all she does. She is often aware that the child is likely to recover; she has hope in the effectiveness of medication and her own loving care; she draws on her long experience of caring for her sick children and her trust in the healing process. So it is with the healing God. In the very process of compassionate sharing of affliction, God is offering healing and hope through many possibilities.

And the way this is achieved is through the action of God's Spirit. Even if it seems that conflict and killing are prevailing, still the Spirit continues to "sharpen the eyes of those who have eyes to see and ears of those who have ears to hear".[41] Because the Churches of the Arab world—not only those in Egypt—are in desperate need of prophets who can read the past, analyze the present, and point to the future, the activity of the Spirit is to sharpen eyes and ears so as to help people to really discern the moment we are now in. This is precisely what I saw Bishop Thomas doing in Upper Egypt.

Do we need to ask ourselves, Christian communities of the East and West, "where have we been as Christians in the decades of horrific totalitarian repression in Egypt, Libya, Iraq and Syria? Where is our witness and solidarity against Christians in the face of the backlash as some seek to wreak revenge on our heads for our support of these regimes?" Does this mean that we retreat into the ghetto? Or do we have the courage to move into the public place proclaiming the values of the Gospel? This is where the fire of the Spirit is revealed, strengthening those, however few, who do not want to abandon their homelands but are struggling to stay:

The Spirit is poured out on those who realize that no one said it would be easy. The last fifty years have seen a progressive displacement of Christians in the Arab world from positions of wealth, influence, and power brokering. Yet now, Christians are being pushed to the margins and there they are called to a close identification with the Crucified One. The Spirit is strengthening those who are seeing in this new (and horrendously difficult task) a real mission of discipleship.[42]

This mission of discipleship in the context of affliction needs the power of the Spirit to give witness despite the price Christians know they may have to pay. But there is another challenge. The rise of the Islamic Brotherhood in Egypt and the ensuing violence that removed President Morsi have both provoked attacks against Christians—this is not just a challenge for Egypt but for all Middle Eastern countries. This is where the work of the Spirit is urgently needed, leading all Christians—East and

West—into the unknown to build bridges with Islam. Above all else, this is the time to cling to hope:

So open your hearts and your homes tonight,
Throw wide the arms of your pain;
Against all the odds,
Despite all the hurt
Risk the piercing of the wind,
Risk the demands of love.[43]

Notes

1. From a personal conversation with Bishop Thomas, Good Friday, May 2013, in Quosia, Upper Egypt.
2. Kate McIhagga, "Into Egypt", in *The Green Heart of the Snowdrop* (Glasgow: Wild Goose Publications, 2004), p. 95.
3. Hosea 11.1, Matthew 2.13–15.
4. This figure is disputed: the number may be higher, but there has not been a census.
5. The main body of the Coptic Church has been out of communion with both the Roman Catholic Church and the various Eastern Orthodox churches for sixteen centuries.
6. Bishop Thomas gave the Annual *Embrace the Middle East* Lecture on 22 May, 2013 at St James' Church, Piccadilly, London.
7. Acts 15.36–41. Mark the evangelist may be also identified with John Mark, but the identification is not certain.
8. <http://en.wikipedia.org/wiki/Mark_the_Evangelist>.
9. See Joseph MacRory, "St Mark", in *The Catholic Encyclopedia*, vol. 9 (New York: Robert Appleton Company, 1910), <http://www.newadvent.org/cathen/09672c.htm>.
10. Some of the problems are in reconciling the various traditions with the evidence in the Acts of the Apostles. There is a substantial amount of

time between AD 50 and 60 during which the New Testament (Acts of the Apostles) is silent in regard to St Mark and his activity in Egypt.

11. Cyrene is important in the Bible because Simon of Cyrene is related as having carried the cross of Christ to Golgotha (Mark, 15:21). It was known, because of its strong philosophical tradition, as "the Athens of Africa".
12. Zora O'Neill (ed.), *Lonely Planet: Egypt* (London: Lonely Planet Publications, 2012), p. 446.
13. For an extensive account of these legends, see Jill Kamil, *Christianity in the Land of the Pharaohs: The Coptic Orthodox Church* (Cairo: The American University in Cairo Press, 2002), pp. 20–34; Otto F.A. Meinardus, *Two Thousand Years of Coptic Christianity* (Cairo: The American University in Cairo Press, 1999), pp. 14–28.
14. See Jill Kamil, *Christianity in the Land of the Pharaohs*, p. 28. This monastery flourishes today, and is famous for its charitable works.
15. Laurence Freeman, Introduction to Rowan Williams, *Silence and Honey Cakes: the Wisdom of the Desert* (Oxford: Lion Publishing, 2003), p. 10.
16. Ahdaf Soueif, *Cairo, My City, My Revolution* (London: Bloomsbury, 2012), p. 187. © Ahdaf Soueif, 2012.
17. Haroon Siddique, "Gaza crisis: Talks continue as Palestinian death toll approaches 700—as it happened", *The Guardian* (23 July 2013), <http://www.theguardian.com/world/2014/jul/23/gaza-crisis-plo-supports-hamas-conditions-for-ceasefire-live-updates>.
18. At the time of writing, May 2014, he is the most likely candidate to become president in the forthcoming elections.
19. Siddique, "Gaza crisis".
20. Patrick Kingsley and Martin Chulov, "Mohamed Morsi ousted in Egypt's second revolution in two years", *The Guardian* (3 July 2013), <http://www.theguardian.com/world/2013/jul/03/mohamed-morsi-egypt-second-revolution>.
21. Jason Howerton, "President Obama: I am 'deeply concerned' by the military takeover in Egypt", *The Blaze* (3 July 2013), <http://www.theblaze.com/stories/2013/07/03/president-obama-i-am-deeply-concerned-by-the-military-takeover-in-egypt>.
22. Kingsley and Chulov, "Mohamed Morsi".
23. "Alexandria church bomb: Egypt police on high alert", BBC News (3 January 2012), <http://www.bbc.co.uk/news/world-middle-east-12107084>.

24. The building was located in the village of Fanous, in the Tamia district of Fayoum province, 130 kilometres south west of Cairo.
25. As reported by David D. Kirkpatrick and Karen Fahim, "Attack on Christians in Egypt Comes After a Pledge", *The New York Times* (8 April 2013).
26. Ibid.
27. A tearful crowd of thousands that included members of Egypt's emerging political class had attended a funeral service for Pope Shenouda III, who spent four decades as the popular and charismatic leader of the Coptic Orthodox Church. The death of the only pope many Egyptian Copts had ever known underscored feelings of unease many Christians have about the tumult of Egypt's political transition since the fall of President Hosni Mubarak. By the early evening, there were scenes of pandemonium as thousands of people mobbed a van carrying Shenouda to his burial site in a monastery in northern Egypt. Red-faced military policemen wrestled mourners carrying the pope's portraits as they strained for a last glimpse through the dark windows of the white van.
28. "Egypt: Pope Tawadros rebukes Morsi over Cathedral clash", BBC News (9 April 2013), <http://www.bbc.co.uk/news/world-middle-east-22083168>.
29. Evan Hill, "Egypt's Christians under Attack", Aljazeera America (21 August, 2013), <http://america.aljazeera.com/articles/2013/8/21/egypt-s-christiansunderattack.html>.
30. Coptic leaders were included on the panel charged with drafting the Constitution but eventually quit, realising that most of their collaborators seemed intent on creating an Islamic state intolerant of minorities.
31. "Egypt—Country profile", from *Aid to the Church in Need* at <http://www.acnuk.org/countries.php/39/Egypt>.
32. Ibid.
33. This section owes much to the ACN Report, *Persecuted but not Forgotten* (December 2013), pp. 48–59.
34. Ibid.
35. Ibid.
36. Ibid.
37. Abigail Frymann, "Egyptian bishop voices hopes for new constitution", in *The Tablet* (21 December 2013). Reproduced with permission of the publisher; <http://www.thetablet.co.uk>.

38. Ibid.
39. An account of some of these incidents is recorded in *Persecuted but not Forgotten*, Appendix A, pp. 49–59.
40. *Persecuted but not Forgotten*, p. 49.
41. I am grateful here for the insights of Fr David Neuhaus, the Roman Catholic Latin Patriarchal Vicar, Jerusalem, in a personal email (8 December 2013).
42. Ibid. Fr Neuhaus continues: "Not every Christian who suffers or, God forbid, dies is a martyr. We are tending to turn every Christian into a martyr, forgetting that a martyr is one who in life and death bears witness and is willing to pray the price. Martyrdom is not just a consequence of following Christ but is a condition of following Christ. Yet Jesus promises that exactly then, the Spirit is given. The Spirit is very much at work!"
43. Kate McIlhagga, "Into Egypt", p. 96. Copyright © Donald McIlhagga.

CHAPTER 5

Breaking the impasse I: The Holy Spirit as bridge-building and creating dialogue.

> Then Paul answered, "What are you doing, weeping and breaking my heart? For I am ready not only to be bound but even to die in Jerusalem for the sake of the Lord Jesus".
>
> *Acts 21.13*

> Dialogue is a spiritual attitude before anything else in which the individual stands before God and talks to Him; thus his self is sublimated and heart and emotions purged . . . Dialogue is a spiritual state that carries us from isolation to absorption, from rejection to acceptance, from labelling to understanding, from distortion to respect . . . [1]

Figure 4: Ofer Prison, November 2013 (near Ramallah).[2]

Imprisonment as experience of the early disciples

It is now time to return to the journeys of Paul, bringing him again to centre-stage. We had left Paul in Damascus after his dramatic conversion (Acts 9). Since then, after the growth of the Church at Antioch, Paul had set sail for Cyprus and begun his missionary work through Asia Minor, always returning to Antioch as his base, then journeying through Syria and Cilicia to strengthen the community of believers (Acts 15.41). Responding to the call of the Macedonians, "Come over to Macedonia to help us!", Paul—with Silas—set sail and arrived in Philippi (Acts 16.9–12). During this visit both he and Silas were flung into prison, eventually being released after the conversion of the gaoler. Being imprisoned for the proclamation of the Gospel became a frequent occurrence for the early disciples. Now Paul was resolved—through the Spirit's guidance—to journey through Macedonia, back to Jerusalem, and then to Rome. Arriving in Jerusalem, he was warmly welcomed by the Christian community, but, after some disturbances, Paul was then dragged out of the temple and arrested (Acts 21.17–36). Thus began his long process of imprisonment and trial—with its eventual ending in Rome (Acts 21–28).

Imprisonment of Palestinians today

Recalling us to the present, this chapter begins its discussion outside a contemporary prison, Camp Ofer. The picture above was taken at a vigil outside the prison by participants of the Sabeel Conference, November 2013. Camp Ofer was originally founded in December 1968, at the location of a former Jordanian Army base from before the Six-Day War. It was named after Lieutenant Colonel Zvi Ofer, the commander of the Haruv Reconnaissance Unit, who was killed in action earlier in the same year. The prison was built in the base in 1988, after the beginning of the First Intifada. Following the Oslo Accords, and the numerous prisoner releases of 1995, Ofer's remaining prisoners and detainees were moved to Megiddo Prison, and Ofer was closed, but was officially re-opened on 29 March 2002 as a response to Operation Defensive Shield.[3]

On 3 October 2006, control of Ofer Prison was moved to the Israel Prison Service (IPS), making it the last incarceration facility for Palestinians to be moved to the IPS (although two detention centres in the West Bank are still controlled by the Military Police Corps). It is still one of Israel's most notorious prisons, and is known for practices of torture perpetrated against Palestinian inmates.

One of the most horrendous practices in Ofer Prison is the incarceration of children. This is reported by non-governmental organizations such as Machsom Watch, who have continuously recorded the imprisonment of children in Ofer Prison.[4] A delegation of British MPs visiting the facilities described the human rights abuses they witnessed:

> The children came in handcuffed with their hands in front of them but all too often their hands are cuffed behind their backs.[5]

Still more disturbing observations were made by a delegation of leading British lawyers who also visited the facilities and observed the use of iron shackles on children, which they considered to be in breach of Article 40 of the UN Convention on the Rights of the Child and the UN Standard Minimum Rules.[6] It is estimated that between 500 and 700 children are arrested each year.[7] Arrests of children emerge at friction points, such as illegal settlements built near Palestinian villages, writes Gerard Horton:

> At these points of frictions demonstrations, arrests and stone-throwing frequently occur, as people vent their frustration against military occupation and the wholesale disregard for the rule of law.[8]

The humiliation and suffering of the children after arrest is painful to relate:

> Many children report being verbally abused and/or physically assaulted whilst being transferred in the back of vehicles . . . any request to use the toilet or for a drink

> of water is usually met with a slap or verbal insult ... Sometime after dawn, the child, now terrified, bruised and sleep deprived, will arrive at a police station inside one of the settlements and so the interrogation phase will begin.[9]

There are numerous testimonies from children and their mothers, and now even soldiers, from the group *Breaking the Silence* who have courageously decided to expose the reality of daily life under the Occupation, and especially the brutality of the prison system.

But, as the authors of *Stolen Youth* relate, this brutal incarceration of children should be looked at within the wider context of Occupation.[10] Israel has always argued that its brutal practices and repressive policies are necessary for "security" in the face of the threat of "terrorism". Yet the vast majority of detained children pose no threat to anyone. The truth is that, "all Palestinian children are subject to the institutionalized discrimination that lies at the heart of Israel's Occupation".[11]

Each phase of the system forms part of a coercive process designed to extract quick confessions, recruit collaborators, demonstrate the overwhelming reach of state power, and force Palestinians into submitting to Israeli control of their land, their resources and their lives.

The problem is also, the authors continue, that attorneys struggling to represent these detained children are essentially powerless, reduced to "damage control" involving some mitigation and plea bargaining.[12] By imprisoning children, Israel sends a message that no one is beyond reach. Nor have the international mechanisms that should ensure compliance with international law offered any protection. There appears to be a conscious political decision not to act against Israel's violations, reflecting undeniable double standards in the international legal system.[13] Finally, the use of political prisoners as "bargaining chips" appears to be a political strategy in any "peace process" that Israel will not easily relinquish.

This was the background to the situation confronting Sabeel pilgrims on that November day in 2013 as we kept vigil outside the Ofer prison. In my mind was the contrast with St Paul and other early disciples who were imprisoned so many centuries ago for witnessing to the Gospel; and now, also inspired by Scripture, we witnessed the continuing injustice inflicted on imprisoned Palestinian children. We kept a silence of shock, anger, and grief. Then we sang, summoning all the hope in our hearts, and with a great voice we pierced the skies: "We shall overcome . . . one day."

Turning to the Spirit

Given the gravity of the current situation in the Occupied territories, what is the guarantee that turning to the Spirit will make any helpful impact and contribution? Speaking as a Roman Catholic, the significant developments of the last fifty years since the Second Vatican Council have been both helpful and illuminating. We, in the Roman Catholic Church, have begun to understand that our theology was overly focused on Christ—*Christomonism,* as it was named.[14] The Holy Spirit had slowly slipped into the background, so much so that a journalist, the late Gerald Priestland (an atheist who became a Quaker), could write a chapter on the Holy Spirit, evoking this loss, entitled, "The Ghost that came to dinner",—the Ghost in question not only came to dinner but stayed on to become a member of the family.[15] He confesses that he approaches the doctrine of the Holy Spirit as "the most exploited and abused piece in the Christian armoury."[16] Priestland means that the Spirit is often called upon as a substitute for credibility and objective discussion, or is assumed to be a vague presence. This low profile meant that not only was the power of the Spirit missing in faith life, but that our understanding of the Holy Trinity itself had become impoverished in Christian understanding. Priestland ends with the intuition that the Spirit was at work before Christ and in other religions—a hotly disputed topic ecumenically.[17]

A loss of the Spirit also meant that a valuable bridge to a shared understanding of the Spirit in Christianity, Islam, and Judaism had been overlooked. Of course, this has not been the case in all Christian denominations, yet it illustrates the chasm between Eastern and Western theologies. The Orthodox Churches have always preserved a rich theology of the Holy Spirit and Trinity, especially in worship. And in the West itself, the Quaker movement in its prayer has always focused on the Spirit. Then, in the late sixties, the emerging charismatic movement gained force and reached out to all Christian denominations to recover the power of the Spirit. If we ask why the emphasis on the Spirit has become so important, the answer is that it acts not only as a bridge to interfaith dialogue with other religions, but because it is through the power of the Spirit that we are brought to God. As Kilian McDonnell put it, the Spirit is the point of departure of our journey to God.[18] I take heart in this understanding of the Spirit from the words of Jesus himself at the Last Supper, when he said that the Spirit would not only remind us of his words and teachings, but would "Guide [us] into truth . . . and he will declare to you the things that are to come" (John 16.13).

There has been a more radical shift to the Holy Spirit "in the post-9/11, multicultural, globalized, inter-faith era".[19] Many theologians—such as Kirsteen Kim and Michael Barnes SJ—have emphasized that this is a helpful step in interfaith relations.[20] So this book has begun with the Gentile Pentecost (Acts 10) which inspired Peter by the revelation that the Spirit is poured out on all humanity, not only on Israel: this led us to contemporary experiences in Gaza, Syria, and Egypt. We have witnessed there how the Holy Spirit is experienced through affliction. And in this current conflict situation, Christians in the Holy Land experience and share the same affliction.

Before exploring how the Spirit is experienced in Judaism and Islam today—as a step towards interfaith understanding—it is vital to understand that the Spirit was definitely not experienced in Jewish history for the first time at the Pentecost event. The Jewish believers who had travelled from so many countries to experience Passover and Pentecost in Jerusalem, who experienced this outpouring knew that the Holy Spirit had been active since the dawn of time. The Spirit brooded over the waters at the moment of creation: "While a wind from God swept over the face of the waters" (Genesis 1.1). The Spirit is the breath of life throughout all Creation, animating all forms of life, pouring out the energy that sustains hope for the future. As the well-loved Psalm 104 (v. 30) says:

> When you send forth your spirit they are created;
> And you renew the face of the ground.

At the same time, the Spirit is the power inspiring the prophets to speak the word of God in times of emergency and distress for the Jewish people. We are familiar with the words of Isaiah (61.1–2):

> The Spirit of the Lord God is upon me,
> Because the Lord has anointed me:
> He has sent me to bring good news to the oppressed,
> To bind up the broken-hearted,
> To proclaim liberty to the captives,
> And release the prisoners.

We are also told that Jesus, steeped in the influence of Isaiah and filled with the power of the Spirit, began his ministry in Nazareth with the same text, and put the concerns of justice expressed by Isaiah at its very heart. This serves as our inspiration today to become more aware that the power of the Holy Spirit works for justice, liberation, and peace in the midst of affliction.

In Chapter 2, I wrote of the Holy Spirit in terms of mutuality, of inspiring epiphanies of connection; I described the Spirit in terms of being the great reconciler and the medium of restorative justice. Now it is time to explore how a shared understanding of the Spirit can help us to make new reconciling connections with both Muslims and Israelis in this time of affliction. And, concerning Islam, Christians do not begin with a vacuum but with both a shared theological understanding and, in Palestine, a shared life experience.

The Holy Spirit in Islam and in Palestinian life today

There is a richness of faith in the Spirit that characterizes traditional Islamic faith. The Spirit of Allah, *al-Ruh*, is used in the Qu'ran with two meanings. First, Allah the Almighty uses the Spirit to blow the spirits or souls of human beings into mothers' wombs. Thus, as with Hebrew Scripture, the Spirit is integral to the creation of life:

> But He fashioned him in due proportion, and breathed into him something of His Spirit. And He gave you [the faculties of] hearing and sight and feeling [and understanding]: little thanks do ye give![21]

And again:

> When I have fashioned him [in due proportion] and breathed into him of *My Spirit*, fall ye down in obeisance unto him.[22]

It is remarkable that, just as the Gospel of Luke in Christian Scripture underlines how the Spirit was integral to the conception of Jesus in Mary, so too does the Qur'an, evoking the possibility that Mohammad possibly had access to the Christian Bible:

> And [remember] her who guarded her chastity: We breathed into her of *Our Spirit*, and We made her and her son a sign for all peoples . . .[23]
>
> And Mary the daughter of 'Imran, who guarded her chastity; and We breathed into [her body] of *Our Spirit*; and she testified to the truth of the words of her Lord and of His Revelations, and was one of the devout [servants].[24]

The second common dimension is how—as in Hebrew and Christian Scriptures—the Spirit is used to provide Divine Guidance to the Believers, those whom Allah Almighty loves and favours. It not only the Holy Spirit that gives guidance, angels also play a role. Finally, those who believe and are strengthened by the Spirit will be admitted to "Gardens beneath which rivers flow."[25]

Thus Dialogue between Christian and Muslim in Palestine already has great depth:

> A common language and common history unites us; there are no social, behavioural or ethical differences between Arab Christians and their brothers, Arab Muslims.[26]

Geries Khoury argues that dialogue between Muslim is not new, but is "nourishment to a tree whose roots go deep in history".[27] It is a dialogue of life shared on many levels. He points out that this dialogue existed as far back as the time of the Prophet Mohammad (who died in 632), enduring through the period of the Caliphate and after.[28] Cultural cooperation continued when Christians and Muslims together faced the Turks under the Ottoman Empire. Fr Rafiq Khoury stresses this cultural cooperation: Eastern Christians translated major parts of the Hellenistic culture of the region into Arabic.[29] It was very common at this time for a Muslim philosopher to be the disciple of a Christian one and vice versa. This was not only the formation of an Arab-Muslim culture, but the development of original Christian thought in Arabic in several religious fields.[30]

This positive picture has not been unaffected by recent events on both the local and international scene. How could Palestinian Muslim-Christian relations remain unaffected by the consequences of the Iraq and Afghan wars, the rise of fundamentalist and radical Islam, and now the tragic situation in Syria where numerous groups of jihadis have joined the rebels against the (Sunni) government forces? The Revd Nadim Nassar, Director of the Awareness Foundation in London, and a Syrian Anglican priest, explained the impact of recent events in Syria; having described the good relationships between the minorities and the Sunni majority (see p. 46) he went on to say:

> In the two years since the conflict began, Syrian minorities, especially Christians, have suffered a great deal. Churches have been deliberately destroyed, Christians have been forced out of their homes, their businesses and their communities, and many have been kidnapped or killed. A great friend of mine, Metropolitan Boulos Yazigi of Aleppo, and his friend Bishop Yohanna Ibrahim, were kidnapped in April.[31]

In the face of these recent events, groups in Palestine/Israel in the context of Muslim-Christian relations have not stood still. In particular, the Sabeel Centre in Jerusalem and Al-Liqa in Bethlehem have tirelessly organised many initiatives. The Eastern Catholic Patriarchs—cited at the beginning of this chapter—have also published moving pastoral letters.[32] The Arab Working Group on Muslim Christian Dialogue, bravely confronting the current problems, published an important document in 2002, entitled *Dialogue and Co-existence: An Arab Muslim-Christian Covenant*.[33]

As Nassar now writes, in the context of the Geneva Peace talks (January 2013), the urgency of the situation no longer lies just with bridge-building with Islam, but in facing the violence of extreme jihadis:

> As the international conference works in Geneva to find a solution for the conflict that is destroying the cradle of civilisation, the world must make sure that the Syrian people in this conference have their best chance in the peace process. But this will not be the end of the violence: those thousands of Jihadists fighting in Syria still remain the biggest challenge that both sides in the peace process have to deal with. Once the war ends, the Jihadists will not meekly pack up their belongings and leave; they are not under the command of the opposition. They are there to die or to establish an Islamic state, and no peace process could satisfy them.[34]

Nassar makes the stakes of this challenge crystal clear: it is a matter of life or death.

Jewish-Christian dialogue: complexities and barriers

It is well-known that fruitful dialogue relies on a supportive context. But how different is the context in Western Europe from that in Palestine/Israel! In my earlier theological studies, a major strand I encountered was Christian responsibility for, or even collusion with, the tragedy of the Holocaust/Shoah. Slowly Christian theologians began to unravel centuries of anti-Judaism in Christian theology, a tradition which began with blaming the Jews for the killing of Jesus and their refusing to accept his new revelation which led to a deep-rooted anti-Semitism in Christian society.[35] Christians had to unlearn so many centuries of false assumptions within a supersessionist theology which gave no place to Jews after the coming of Christ. The phrase "the perfidious Jews" was then eliminated from the Good Friday liturgy in the Catholic Church. The Constitution of Vatican II, *Nostra Aetate*, was firm in restoring rightful dignity to Judaism and Islam: together with Christianity, they are the three Abrahamic faiths.[36] Jewish-Christian dialogue has gone from strength to strength, with valuable work being achieved by, for example, the Council of Christians and Jews on an international level. Yet the struggle against anti-Semitism is by no means overcome as new occurrences are continually experienced in many different countries.

But the context for dialogue in Palestine/Israel could not be more different. As Father David Neuhaus writes (emphasis is mine):

> In the Middle East today, Jews are not generally perceived as victims of marginalization and persecution but rather as the face of a problematic political reality in the Middle East *in the form of the State of Israel and its occupation of Palestinian lands.*[37]

Is the continuing sense of guilt over the Holocaust and the legacy of anti-Semitism obscuring the worsening suffering of Palestinians and their legitimate demand for justice? Is it part of the problem (referred to earlier in the discussion of the abuses witnessed in Israeli prisons) of the double standards allowed to the Israelis internationally? Sadly, the answer must be "yes". Contemporary efforts to raise awareness of the Palestinian situation are frequently victim to new accusations of anti-Semitism. For example, in December 2013, a campaign called "Bethlehem Unwrapped" was enacted outside St James' Church in Piccadilly, London. Here the Separation Wall was erected outside the church and used as a backcloth for a variety of events—music, festivity, and speeches. The campaign—supported by many charities—was organised to demonstrate how the real separation barrier, a construction that has been deemed to be illegal under international law:

> [The Wall] is impacting the lives of millions of Palestinians. These include many indigenous Christians in Bethlehem, whose historic lands have been confiscated for the barrier.[38]

This dramatic event attracted a staggering degree of positive support, awaking the consciousness of many people to the plight of the Palestinians; equally, and sadly, it garnered numerous accusations of anti-Semitism. In a letter to the *Church Times*, Jeremy Moodey, the Chief Executive of the NGO *Embrace the Middle East*, responded to a leading article in a preceding issue of the same journal criticising the *Bethlehem Unwrapped* project and the Rector of St James, Revd Lucy Winkett, in the context of anti-Semitism; he succinctly pointed out that:

> The battle against genuine anti-Semitism is devalued when it is widened to include non-violent campaigns to persuade the State of Israel to comply with its obligations under international law.[39]

Of course, there needs to be continuing and genuine sensitivity to the fact that the global Jewish population will continue to grieve over the terrible genocide inflicted upon their people by the Nazis during the Second World War; this is rightly remembered with empathy by the entire world on, for example, Holocaust Day, and the tragedy and its consequences taught to the children of the next generation. But today's Palestinian people should not be punished because of what had been inflicted on Jews by the Nazi Government!

Contrary to what one might expect, the fact that Palestinian Christians share the Bible with the Jewish people is not an advantage in this situation. Sadly for Palestinians Christians, the Bible has been used as a foundation text by the Israelis to justify taking possession of Palestinian land:

Zionism, the ideology of Jewish nationalism, often reads the Bible as a legal, historical or even divinely revealed title deed to the land . . . This is particularly evident in certain forms of Christian Zionism that offer Biblical justification for the dispossession of the Palestinians and hostility toward Muslims.[40]

This means that the Jewish foundational text of the Book of Exodus, the story of the oppressed Israelites leaving Egypt for the desert and, ultimately, the Promised Land (celebrated annually at the Jewish Passover) cannot be experienced as liberation by the Palestinians, who face the reality of losing their land every day. It is felt with great sadness that the Bible has been "colonised" to allow the daily suffering of the Palestinians.[41]

Yet even within these blockages, Fr David Neuhaus makes concrete suggestions.[42] First, he encourages a dialogue of daily life: Jews, Christians, and Muslims already come together in various NGOs with a shared search for justice, peace and, reconciliation. Neuhaus adds an urgent plea that this coming together of the three groups should not ignore spiritual aspects. Theology and spirituality should never be left to fanatics and fundamentalists! Secondly, he calls for a shared study of the Bible. I would add that the theme of redemptive violence should be challenged as being damaging to Jews and Christians alike. This is a frequent reading of the Bible which justifies murder and killing as being an inevitable part of the redemptive plan. Thirdly, Neuhaus would like to invite Jews and Christians to remember a time when Jews lived integrated within the Middle Eastern peoples. Not only does he mean that before 1948 Jewish Arabs were as significant part of the Middle East, as were Christian Arabs, but that they made a significant contribution to Arab culture. All three religions, he says finally, are called to lives of faith and hope.

This appeal finds resonance in many hopeful initiatives. For example, Lucy Nusseibeh, Director of the NGO *Middle East Non-Violent Democracy* (MEND),[43] who lives in Jerusalem, addressed the difficulty of dialogue in a conflict situation in a lecture given at Caux, Switzerland:

> People in a conflict need to be encouraged to make every effort to maintain their human connectivity, even perhaps taught to consciously cultivate empathy in order precisely to overcome the dehumanising and polarizing effects of the conflict and create a possible space for peace.[44]

She highlighted that in a situation where both societies are traumatized, for different historical reasons, the demonization in conflicts targets the entire population, tending to dismiss the possibility of any "innocents", so that all become enemies and all are casualties. In such a situation, the need to promote empathy and rebuild trust is not only imperative it is urgent. Nusseibeh also discussed the obstacles to dialogue and to peace: people's own unconscious defence mechanisms and the problems of dwelling on wrongs and suffering. She stressed that, by looking in the mirror with an awareness and acknowledgement of our own wrong-doing, we must accept that we are perpetrators as well as victims, but that we can create space for deeper dialogue and true understanding, and pave a way for peace. Sadly, she reflected, especially since the war in Gaza, only a handful of people are ready to commit to dialogue. Both societies are traumatized, entrenched in a siege mentality and stuck in a mind-set of victimhood. This is a mind-set that projects all the evil onto the "other", the perceived enemy, and denies culpability for any evil in the sufferer. It makes it impossible for someone who is suffering and sees him/herself as a victim to also acknowledge that they themselves also cause suffering. But, of course, in conflicts, whether between individuals or between peoples or countries, *people tend to be both victims and perpetrators.*[45] These thoughts, fears, and actions create further reasons for people to have no contact and to refuse intercultural dialogue. The mind-set of suffering or victimhood therefore blocks out any possibility of dialogue.

One might wonder, then, what does Nusseibeh suggest as a way forward? One way to deal with it, she argues, is to bring these deep-seated attitudes and feelings into consciousness. By reflection and awareness of the fact that none of us are entirely virtuous, we start to free up space in this cycle of dehumanization. I suggest that here we are in the realm of the reconciling Spirit's work. What gives heart to our understanding about how the Spirit works in affliction is the way some Israeli NGOs are also struggling to raise awareness of the truth of the situation. One of these NGOs is *Zochrot*:

> *Zochrot* and other Israeli NGOs have been fairly successful over the past few years in raising the *Nakba* to the awareness of the broad Jewish public. The destruction of hundreds of villages and resulting hundreds of thousands of Palestinian refugees in the 1948 War have become part and parcel of current Israeli discourse; nevertheless, its mere presence

> in Jewish Israeli discourse still does not mean broad acknowledgement of and accountability for the *Nakba*. This gap is largely due to the continued adherence of Jewish Israeli society to colonial concepts and practices.[46]

Zochrot believes that peace will come only after the country has been decolonized, enabling all its inhabitants and refugees to live together without the threat of expulsion or denial of Return.[47] *Zochrot* also believes strongly in the Right of Return of the refugees:

> Zochrot envisions Return as an extended and multidimensional process, which includes not only the physical return of refugees to this country, but also their appropriate and dignified integration in an equal, joint Palestinian-Jewish society. Under this expansive view, Return begins long before the actual return of refugees and proceeds long after.[48]

The vision of *Zochrot* is that the return of the Palestinian refugees to their country will be on the basis of acknowledgement and accountability, coupled with a joint Jewish-Palestinian process of restitution founded on the principles of transitional justice. This Return will be a central and essential part of the creation of a multicultural democratic space and a joint and equitable fabric of life for all inhabitants of this country on all levels (from home and neighborhood to state level) and in all sectors (economics, politics, and urban planning, but also education, arts, and sports). *Zochrot* realizes the necessity of acknowledging the truth of the *Nakba* in Israeli society:

> To realize its vision, *Zochrot* will act to promote Israeli Jewish society's acknowledgement of and accountability for the ongoing injustices of the *Nakba* and the reconceptualization of Return as the imperative redress of the Nakba and a chance for a better life for all the country's inhabitants, so that it renounces the colonial conception of its existence in the region and the colonial practices it entails.[49]

These two examples, MEND and Zochrot, have been cited—among many possible others—to demonstrate how the Holy Spirit works across boundaries and towards a non-violent response to the conflict. Acknowledging truth, coming to terms with the possibility that we are both victim and perpetrator, is one way to cross over to the reality of the demonized "other". But in order not to fall into the trap of overlooking that there is still worsening oppression of the Palestinians, even if Israelis may be suffering from post-traumatic stress disorder,[50] we must respond to the fact that the Spirit is a Spirit of liberation. This is the inspiration of Samuel Rayan, an Indian theologian, who founds his whole theology on the mission of the Spirit.[51] The Spirit is the breath of fire, coming to enable us to re-create our world. Fire invokes judgment and revolution and is fearful and uncontrollable.[52] Rayan pioneered a spirituality of liberation in India; in a context of the Eucharist, he declares:

> Our task is . . . to communicate the One Spirit who impels to justice and liberate the downtrodden and to invite men and women to come and taste the One Bread or rice-bowl of life which all of us are to become and break with one another.[53]

Rayan's appeal to the Spirit of liberation is situated in a context of pluralism. He sees religions (which are, in his context, Hinduism, Islam, Sikhism, and Buddhism) as "joint creation of the Spirit and Spirit experience of human groups"; mystery, he declares, is only expressible through a thousand mediations.[54] But, lest the impression be given that this spirituality lapses into an otherworldly mysticism, I must stress that Rayan's vision of the Spirit is one of fullness of life for all, beginning with the downtrodden.

Samuel Rayan's vision opens a window to the way the Holy Spirit both enables bridge-crossing to the experience of other faiths in context of conflict; it also helps in keeping our focus most keenly on those most oppressed and suffering. Beginning with Paul's experience of imprisonment, and bringing it into comparison with the contemporary suffering of Palestinian children, this chapter has opened us to a wider experience of the Holy Spirit, crossing over boundaries and inviting to new understandings. But one dimension has been overlooked: how does the experience of women in this conflict affect and deepen the understanding of how the Spirit works?

Notes

1. Eastern Catholic Patriarchs, cited in Geries Khoury, "Christian-Muslim Dialog in the Holy Land", in *Cornerstone*, Issue 64 (Winter 2012), p. 5.
2. All photographs, unless otherwise stated, by the author.
3. Operation *Defensive Shield* was a large-scale military operation conducted by the Israel Defense Forces in 2002, during the course of the Second Intifada. It was the largest military operation in the West Bank since the 1967 Six-Day War. The operation was an attempt by the Israeli army to stop the increasing deaths from terrorist attacks, especially in suicide bombings. The spark that gave rise to the action was the 27 March suicide bombing during Passover Seder at the Park Hotel in the Israeli resort city of Netanya; a Palestinian suicide bomber killed 30, mostly elderly, vacationers; see <http://en.wikipedia.org/wiki/Operation_Defensive_Shield>.
4. The daily reports can be access at <http://www.machsomwatch.org/en/daily-reports/military-courts/Ofer>.
5. Richard Burden as quoted in Amira Hass, "Otherwise Occupied / Labour is concerned", *Ha'aretz* (13 December 2010). Burden was a member of a British Labour Party delegation headed by Labour MP Sandra Osborne which toured the West Bank in 2010.
6. See S. Sedley et al, *Children in Military Custody* (June 2012), available for download at <http://www.childreninmilitarycustody.org>.
7. See Gerard Horton, "Breaking a Generation: Children in Military Detention", *Cornerstone*, 63 (Summer and Fall 2012), pp. 1–4.
8. Ibid., p. 2.
9. Ibid., pp. 2–3
10. See Catherine Cook, Adam Hanien, and Adam Kay, *Stolen Youth: the Politics of Israel's Detention of Palestinian Children*, (London: Pluto Press, 2004), pp. 7–10, and p. 162.

11. Ibid., p. 163.
12. Ibid., p. 164.
13. Ibid., p. 165.
14. For example, by the Russian theologian Vladimir Lossky. Lossky and others thought that the one-sided nature of Western theology should be counterbalanced by the development of pneumatology, and that the Orthodox churches should contribute their own pneumatology to ecumenical discussions. See Kirsteen Kim, *The Holy Spirit in the World—A Global Conversation* (London: SPCK, 2007), p. 44.
15. Gerald Priestland, *Priestland's Progress: One Man's Search for Christianity Now* (London: Ariel Books, 1983), pp. 106–119.
16. Ibid., p. 106.
17. Ibid., p. 119.
18. Kilian McDonnell, *The Other Hand of God: The Holy Spirit as the Universal Touch and Goal* (Collegeville: Liturgical Press, 2003), pp. 111–115.
19. Dermot Lane, *Stepping-Stones to other Religions: a Christian Theology of Inter-Religious Dialogue* (Dublin: Veritas Publications, 2011), p. 169.
20. It is beyond the scope of this book to trace the relations between Spirit and Trinity—important though they be. Along with Dermot Lane, cited above, I see the emphasis on the Spirit as a more helpful starting point for my theme.
21. Qur'an, sura 32 (As-Sajda), ayat 9.
22. Qur'an, sura 15 (Al-Hijr), ayat 29.
23. Qur'an, sura 21 (Al-Anbiya), ayat 91.
24. Qur'an, sura 66 (At-Tahrim), ayat 12.
25. "Thou wilt not find any people who believed in God and the Last Day, loving those who resist God and His Apostle, even though they were their fathers or their sons, or their brothers, or their kindred. For such He has written Faith in their hearts, and strengthened them with a Spirit from Himself. And He will admit them to Gardens beneath which Rivers flow, to dwell therein (forever). God will be well pleased with them, and they with Him. They are the Party of God. Truly it is the Party of God that will achieve Felicity"; Qur'an, sura 58 (Al-Mujadila), ayat 22.
26. Khoury, G., "Christian-Muslim Dialog in the Holy Land", p. 4.
27. Ibid., p. 4.

28. Ibid. He tells us of thousands of manuscripts which exist that could be studied and published providing great wisdom for the international community.
29. Fr Rafiq Khoury, "Living together: the Experience of Muslim-Christian Relations in the Arab world in general and in Palestine in particular", in *Cornerstone*, 64 (Winter 2012), pp. 10–12.
30. This is becoming known to us in the present particularly through the work of the Revd Kenneth Bailey, *Jesus through Middle Eastern Eyes* (London: SPCK, 2008).
31. Nadim Nassar, "Weapons don't stop war", p. 6. The kidnapping of the bishops was referred to in Chapter 3. At the time of writing, the fate of the Bishops is still unknown.
32. See the Pastoral Letter written in Christmas 1994, which was called *Together before God for Human Beings and Society: the living together between Christians and Muslims in the Arab world*; see Fr Rafiq Khoury, "Living together", p. 12.
33. In reference to both the document noted and the pastoral letters of the Eastern Catholic Patriarchs, see Fr Rafiq Khoury, "Living together", pp. 12–13.
34. Nadim Nassar, "Jihad and Geneva", Awareness Foundation (27 January 2014), <http://www.awareness-foundation.co.uk/index.php/nadim/102-jihad-and-geneva>.
35. A helpful resource in this study is Rosemary Radford Ruether's ground-breaking book, *Faith and Fratricide: the Theological roots of anti-Semitism* (New York; The Seabury Press, 1974).
36. See *Nostra Aetate*, in Austin Flannery OP (ed.), *Documents of the Second Vatican Council* (New York: Costello Publishing Company, 1975), pp. 738–742.
37. Fr David Neuhaus, "Christian-Jewish Relations in the Contest of Israel-Palestine", in *Cornerstone,* 64 (Winter 2012), p. 6.
38. Jeremy Moodey, Letter to the *Church Times* (24 January 2014), p. 6.
39. Ibid.
40. Neuhaus, "Christian-Jewish Relations in the Contest of Israel-Palestine", p. 7.
41. This was the theme of the Sabeel Conference, November 2013, in Jerusalem: *The Bible and the Palestine-Israel Conflict.*

42. Neuhaus, "Christian-Jewish Relations in the Contest of Israel-Palestine", p. 8.
43. MEND promotes active nonviolence and encourages alternatives to violence among youth and adults throughout Palestine. MEND employs innovative methods, especially with the media, and is widely respected for working with authenticity, professionalism and courage; see <http://www.mendonline.org>.
44. Lucy Nusseibeh, "Deepening cultural dialogue and understanding", <http://www.mendonline.org/InterculturalDialogue2009.html>.
45. 45 Lucy Nusseibeh, Lecture given at Caux, Switzerand for an *Initiatives of Change* Conference, 21 July 2009. She continues: "A sense of victimhood promotes self-righteousness to the extent that it tends to deny the evil in the victim and project it onto the other, making them into a monster, the embodiment of evil, and it tends to make the victim, regardless of their actual actions, see themselves as totally innocent in all their actions. Violent acts therefore cannot be perceived as such and therefore there is no perceived need for empathy or for finding a middle ground."
46. <http://www.zochrot.org/en/>.
47. "*Zochrot* includes both women and men. We chose the name because we believed that the way Israelis remember the 1948 war is fundamentally militaristic and chauvinistic in nature, focusing primarily on battles, operations, conquests, and heroism. We chose a verb tense less frequently employed in Hebrew as an expression of our attempt to create a feminist alternative addressing other topics, such as the lives of Palestinian communities living in Israel before the war and the fate of their women, their men and their children", <http://zochrot.org/en/contentAccordion/fAQ>.
48. Taken from the "Who we are" section of the Zochrot website; see <http://zochrot.org>. I realise there are many other NGOs with similar aims, such as *Rabbis for Human Rights, Gush Shalom*, etc.
49. Ibid. Furthermore, "*Zochrot* will act to challenge the Israeli Jewish public's preconceptions and promote awareness, political and cultural change within it to create the conditions for the Return of Palestinian Refugees and a shared life in this country. To do so, *Zochrot* will generate processes in which Israeli Jews will reflect on and review their identity, history, future and the resulting discourse through which they conceive of their lives

in this country. Our focus on the Jewish target audience derives from its practical and moral responsibility for Palestinian refugeehood, as well as from its privileged power position under the present regime."

50. Such is the opinion of Rabbi Michael Lerner; see Rabbi Michael Lerner, *Embracing Israel-Palestine* (San Francisco: Tikkun Books, 2011), pp. 261–262.
51. Samuel Rayan, *The Holy Spirit—Heart of the Christian Gospel* (Maryknoll: Orbis, 1978), cited in Kirsteen Kim, *The Holy Spirit in the World: a Global Conversation* (Maryknoll: Orbis, 2007), pp. 87–95.
52. Ibid., p. 91.
53. Samuel Rayan, "Baptism and conversion: the Lima text in the India context", in Godwin Singh (ed.), *A Call to Discipleship*, (Delhi: ISPCK, 1985), pp. 167–187, as cited in Kim, *The Holy Spirit in the World*, p. 92.
54. Kim,*The Holy Spirit in the World*, p. 92.

CHAPTER 6

Breaking the impasse II: The experience of women and the Holy Spirit as beauty

> Flow backwards to your sources, sacred rivers,
> And let the world's great order be reversed . . .
> Stories shall now turn my condition to a fair one,
> Women shall now be paid their due.[1]
>
> ***Euripides***

> Powerful imagination is not false outward vision, but intense inward representation, and a creative energy constantly fed by susceptibility to the veriest minutiae of experience.[2]
>
> ***George Eliot***

> We remained in this city [Philippi] some days; and on the Sabbath day we went outside the gate by the river, where we supposed there was a place of prayer; and we sat down and spoke to the women who had come together. A certain woman named Lydia, a worshipper of God was listening to us. She was from the city of Thyatira and a dealer in purple cloth. The Lord opened her heart to listen eagerly to what was said by Paul. And when she and her household were baptized, she urged us, saying, "If you have judged me to be faithful to the Lord, come and stay at my home." And she prevailed upon us.
>
> ***Acts 16.12–15***

What follows is decisive moment in the life and mission of St Paul. Responding to a vision in the night, where a man from Macedon appealed to him, "Come over to Macedon and help us" (Acts 16.9), Paul understood this as a direct call from the Spirit to cross over to Europe for the proclamation of the Gospel. Thus he arrived in Philippi, which was to become an important site for the new Christian community in Macedon. This event it is important in the context of this book for another reason: there are not many situations recorded where the growth of the early communities was facilitated by women. Yes, the ministry of Priscilla, Phoebe, Dorcas (Tabitha), and others are mentioned in the Acts of the Apostles or in Paul's Letters, but the writer of Acts deliberately describes the *group* of women who had assembled at "the place of prayer" outside the town, near the river, and probably in a small house. These women met together, prayed and preached; they sang and praised God, and, as the story relates, also welcomed newcomers and strangers. And so Paul and his friends were also warmly welcomed. One of the women is mentioned by name: Lydia. Her leading role is specifically emphasised, and we learn about her profession and her background. We are told where she comes from—Thyatira, which lay on the border between Lydia and Mysia, and which was famous for the dyeing trade—and how she earns her living. Lydia, and perhaps also some of the other women, is a business woman. In contrast to what would have been expected in her time and culture, Lydia is a leader at work, in her community, and in her household. She sold purple cloth, which in itself was a luxury item for the wealthy, and beautiful to look at, a famous product of the region. But obtaining the purple colour from plants and dyeing the fabric with it was very hard work, a physically demanding and dirty job. Often several women would join together in one business and employ others. Sometimes they lived and worked together in family-like groups called "houses". They came from all sorts of backgrounds—men and women—and they had access to the houses of the "beautiful and wealthy", where they were able to sell their products. We can imagine how the baptism of Lydia and "her household" may have helped Christianity to enter very many different hearts and houses. Under Lydia's leadership, and with the support of Paul and his friends who stayed in Lydia's home for some time, the early church in Philippi became a place for all quarters of society—women, men, children, rich and poor. It was to this burgeoning Christian community that Paul would write one of his most beautiful letters.[3] Thyatira, too, would become a flourishing Christian centre.[4]

Lydia was clearly a person of agency, responsibility, and economic authority. We have no record of her from other sources, nor is she mentioned in Paul's Letters, but she still serves as a witness to the significance of women in the growth of Christianity. She is a symbol, in my mind, of another revelation of the Spirit—that of beauty and imagination. In the previous chapter the focus was on the Holy Spirit as bridge-building, in crossing barriers with understanding and empathy with "the other". Keeping this focus, the development here is to explore how that same empathy can be developed through the Spirit, revealed through beauty, creativity, and imagination—all ingredients of inspiration.

The Holy Spirit revealed as beauty

Readers may find it strange both to associate the Holy Spirit with beauty, in a work where the context is affliction, and to link this specifically with the experience and memories of women (I already alluded to this theme of spirit, beauty, and vision in Chapter 1). I want to emphasize here that in no way do I want to devalue mixed gender groups seeking justice, or the efforts of heroic prophetic men in peace-building. I simply want to bring the efforts and contributions of women who tend still to be marginalized within Middle Eastern cultures out of the shadows and into the light, their efforts unrecognised by outsiders who would otherwise be eager to support the struggle for justice.

But is this theme of beauty and the Spirit something new, or is it already found in Christian tradition? And what could kind of resource is beauty in a context of war and occupation in Palestine?

The first link, in alluding to beauty and the Holy Spirit, is a poetic one, particularly where the poets—especially the Romantics of both the Eastern and Western worlds—have found beauty, nature, and the spirit an inspirational theme. William Wordsworth, for example, often writes of a presence in Nature, sometimes calling this the spirit:

> I felt a sense of pain when I beheld the silent trees, and saw the intruding sky—then, dearest Maiden, move along these shades in gentleness of heart; with gentle hand touch—for there is a spirit in the woods.[5]

But this is given an explicitly theological meaning by, among others, Gerard Manley Hopkins, a nineteenth-century poet-priest, in the sense of the renewing work of the Holy Spirit in nature, where humanity has wreaked only ruin:

> And for all this, nature is never spent,
> there lives the dearest freshness deep down things;
> and though the last lights off the black West went
> Oh, morning, at the brown brink eastward, springs—
> because the Holy Ghost over the bent
> world broods with warm breast
> and with ah! bright wings.[6]

Yet this theme is far wider than creation as an expression of God's beauty and glory manifested in the Spirit—although this link was abundantly manifest in some of the earliest theologians of the Church. Patrick Sherry noted that Simone Weil's (cited in Chapter 1) attitude towards beauty in the context of affliction was that:

> The beauty of the world is the most likely way to God for people of our time—and she criticized Christianity for having so little to say about it.[7]

Sherry, in his inspiring book *Spirit and Beauty*, widens this theme to include both spiritual and moral beauty. St Irenaeus (the second-century bishop of Lyons) linked the Spirit with wisdom.[8] Dimensions of contemplation, insight, illumination, and realisation contribute to enriching the theme.[9] Further enrichment is offered where Sherry develops a widened concept of inspiration and creativity—a creativity that is more far-reaching than the art galleries, classical music, and poetry beloved of the privileged classes:

> The product of this creativity includes works of art, but also children, crops, gardens, scientific theories, and many other forms of what patent laws calls "intellectual properties".[10]

Inspiration, too, means more than the interpretation given in connection with Old Testament prophecy. It also means the life-giving and transforming communication of the Holy Spirit. The next step is to relate this to imagination. John McIntyre describes the Holy Spirit as God's imagination:

> . . . Let loose and working with all the freedom of God in the world, and in the lives, the words and actions of the men and women of our times.[11]

Sherry writes of *inspired imagination*: one of the functions of this is to seek a deeper truth within our own experience—as George Eliot was hinting in the quotation cited at the beginning of this chapter. This is further deepened by what is called *imagination of the heart*, or moral imagination, as we recognize, in this process of reconciliation, the need for exercising imagination in coming to understand others and cultivating mutual sympathies.[12]

I have now reached the point at which to recall the theology of the Holy Spirit of Nancy Victorin Vangerud (referred to in Chapter 2) in connection with the Gentile Pentecost of Acts 10; she develops a "maternal pneumatology of mutual recognition":[13]

> In contrast to the kyriocentric[14] household management, which domesticates and subordinates the differences of household members, a feminist maternal economy of mutual recognition seeks a "new poetics of community", where differentiation becomes the key to justice, love, and global flourishing.[15]

An economy of *mutual recognition* relates to John Taylor's idea of the Spirit creating "annunciations" (his word for encapsulating I-Thou encounters), with the Spirit acting as the "Go-between God",[16] who draws together the I and Thou towards deeper mutuality. But I also link this with my own work on connectedness: I envision interconnectedness as Divine Epiphany, reaching out beyond the interconnections in the natural world, even though in our own context we begin from such brokenness and exploitation in this respect. Reconnecting is how we recover energy and creativity in the present, in contact with sustaining and nurturing memories from the past.[17] Thus, the late feminist American poet, Adrienne Rich, wrote so inspiringly (emphasis is mine):

> Freedom. It isn't once, to walk out
> under the Milky Way, feeling the rivers
> of light, the fields of dark—
> *freedom is daily, prose-bound, routine*
> *remembering. Putting together, inch by inch*
> *the starry worlds. From all the lost collections.*[18]

Who remembers? How we remember, how the memories are recorded, is the issue. What memories become the official collective memory and what has been silenced? Is it male-structured and male-dominated? Here the position and authority of women in the household is important. It is beyond dispute that Palestinian households—and indeed Middle Eastern households in general—are patriarchal in nature: despite this, women are enormously influential in the household. The social space itself is an open one, encompassing the wider family and even neighbours; here there is normally no segregation of the sexes.[19] Patriarchal culture and traditions bring into play many consequences: they affect women's role in decision-making, in possibilities for access to education, and in marriage arrangements, for example. One hopeful factor of contemporary life in Occupied Palestine is the enthusiastic determination for education among both women and men, even if girls may have problems in finishing secondary education and moving on to the third level, due to early marriage. All the time this is changing, with a younger generation becoming even more committed and determined. An early Arab feminist writer, Anbara Salam Khalidi, born in Beirut but living long years in Palestine, writes of her admiration for Palestinian women's courage and commitment to the struggle:

> I was equally impressed by the zeal for education among Palestinian women . . . Each Palestinian mother took upon herself the education of her children and knew everything there was to know about their educational level and school grades . . .[20]

Equally important is the awareness of the need to hear and value women"s stories. The *Sumud* Story House in Bethlehem has created a space of beauty where women are welcomed and encouraged to tell their stories.[21] In their recent work, "Let me tell you my story", women from four communities in and around Bethlehem—thus including both urban and rural environments—were enabled to speak about human rights issues concerning education, work, health, and domestic violence:

> They . . . suffer from many forms of discriminations and also from restrictive influences of family structures, even though they had more space to develop themselves due to the urban atmosphere of privacy. Visiting the Sumud Story House . . . was for the village and camp women an experience that encouraged them to share their stories more, also outside their communities. "Let me stay and tell you my story" said one of the women from the village on a visit to the House, despite her husband's objections.[22]

But Palestinian women's stories also include memories from the past—in this case focusing on when Palestinians were in possession of their own lands and villages before 1948. Such vital memories are to be handed on to the next generation. Adrienne Rich writes of this significance in another context:

> What would it mean to think
> you are part of a generation
> that simply must pass on?
> What would it mean to live
> in the desert, try to live
> a human life, something

> to hand on to the children
> to take up to the Land?
> What would it mean to think
> you were born in chains and only time,
> nothing you can do
> could redeem the slavery
> you were born into?[23]

Fatma Kassem explores how memory may be gendered in certain ways. Women may have to resist silencing, perhaps due to family pressures, and, if so, especially through brothers and husbands. They may work through many layers of oppression, even to the extent of doubting they have a story to tell. Adrienne Rich warns about this:

> The technology of silence . . .
> Is a presence
> it has a history   a form
> Do not confuse it
> with any kind of absence [24]

In Fatma Kassem's work, which includes interviewing thirty-seven women from the Lydda and Ramle district of Israel and listening to their life stories, she observes that women sometimes use language differently. For example, many women avoid using the word *Nakba* (catastrophe), the official way Palestinians refer to the dispossession of 1948. They believe that this gives a sense of permanence to the current situation, preferring to say simply, "the Jews came".[25] Women's stories focus on their own agency in keeping the family and household going in stressful situations while their husbands and sons may face long imprisonments in Israel gaols, or even if they have died. But in so doing, they manifest the way the Holy Spirit is revealed as beauty. Here I invoke a widened interpretation of beauty, culturally understood. This is beauty experienced in ordinary daily life. It is dependent on intuition, perception, listening, and vision. Again to cite George Eliot (the pen-name of Mary Ann Evans):

> If we had a keen vision and feeling for all ordinary life, it would be like hearing the grass grow and the squirrel's heart-beat, and we should die of that roar that lies on the other side of silence.[26]

Now it is becoming clear why Lydia has become the symbolic matrix for the Holy Spirit as revealed through Beauty in this chapter. Lydia runs a household—we presume—but not on patriarchal lines.[27] She offers hospitality, the same hospitality that is part of present-day Palestinian society. But she is also involved in the creation of something beautiful, the purple cloth, which is also her means of living. This serves to link the experience of contemporary Palestinian women in this conflict situation with the experience of beauty through affliction.

Women's agency is primarily expressed in keeping the household going in spite of the desperate circumstances of ongoing conflict. There is courage, creativity, and beauty involved in feeding and nurturing children, in preparing meals with love and care, in valuing the household and extended family unit. Like Lydia, women in Palestine and across the Middle East negotiate freedom and creativity in a patriarchal culture. In Bethlehem, the Arab Education Centre (AEI) and other groups involve women in creative projects around the illegal Separation Wall, employing music, dance, and theatre productions as expression of protest and resistance, but also as demonstrations of the refusal to allow the creative spirit of beauty to be extinguished by the Occupation. Again, *this is the Holy Spirit being revealed as beauty.*

Fatma Kassem writes of women describing themselves as working ceaselessly in agriculture, baking, sewing, and knitting.[28] Palestinian women also express a love of beauty in their traditional embroidery which has become a cherished language for expression and identity. Anbara Salam Khalidi writes admiringly (in 1978) of the efforts of Palestinian women in reviving the heritage of needlepoint work, and effort which was primarily aimed at relieving the suffering of refugee women; ". . . their work has advanced in quality to the point where their finished products became objects of fine art and fashion".[29]

The most common items are the cross-stitch-embroidered dresses made by village women from natural handmade materials. Their earliest embroidery combines predominantly geometric and abstract patterns (triangles, eight pointed stars, chevrons, squares, lozenges) with some representational motifs, such as flowers and trees. Later, other motifs were introduced as a result of external influences and historical events.

Embroidery for Palestinian women represents a bridge that connects the current context to their history before the diaspora. Here is one of the reasons that they adhere to traditional attire which has powerfully portrayed their style and customs for hundreds of years. Many of the motifs now seen on contemporary Palestinian dresses can also be seen on mosaics and graffiti. Sadly, there are not many examples available to illustrate Palestinian textiles before the last century other than descriptions in memoirs of travellers and the writings of orientalists. In general, the motifs, colours, and themes of Palestinian embroidery have been modified throughout history to reflect lifestyle changes. Costumes for special occasions—especially weddings—were regionally and stylistically diverse, while great emphasis was placed on detail. Visual elements of these costumes reflected a correspondingly detailed system of meaning that centred on identity.[30] Until the end of the Mandate period, most village women made and embroidered their own dresses. In some areas—like Ashdod, Gaza, and the Galilee—women themselves wove and dyed their own fabrics: Lydia's heritage is still alive! While Palestinian women's embroidery can be divided into four categories—ritual, technical, geographic, and structural—the tradition of embroidery in Palestine has revolved around preparations for bridal trousseaus, given that wedding ceremonies are considered to be the most important occasion in the life of the Palestinian family. Of course, this embroidery has been developed in contemporary times to be a resource for living in selling a variety of items, from mobile phone cases to purses, to tourists.

Palestinian women in the contemporary struggle

But let it not be supposed that the witness of Palestinian women to the work of the Holy Spirit is confined solely to creating beauty in the household environment, even if this is at the centre of their lives. There is a long tradition of the involvement of women in the political struggle, especially in the non-violent movement, right back to the days of the British Mandate.[31] Women are making a unique contribution in the area of human rights, fighting for their husbands and sons who have been unjustly imprisoned. They have been involved in peace movements in a variety of ways. As Gila Svirsky observes:

> Ever since Women in Black began its first vigil in 1988, women's peace activism in Israel has consistently been more varied and more progressive than the peace movements of the mixed gender peace groups.[32]

The first Women's Peace Movement was *Women in Black*, which began, as noted above, in 1988, and this has now become a global movement. It was a small Israeli women's group who, wearing black clothes and holding a black sign in the shape of a hand with white letters that said "Stop the Occupation" that was the catalyst for this international movement.[33] This was followed by the *Coalition of Women for Peace*.[34] This group seeks to work together for peace approved a set of principles that included such goals as an end to the occupation, the full involvement of women in negotiations for peace, the recognition of Jerusalem as the shared capital of two states, equality, inclusion, and justice for Palestinian citizens of Israel, and equal rights for women and all citizens of Israel.[35] Despite numerous non-violent actions, there has been very little media interest in this coalition; at least part of this must be attributed to the continuing silencing and marginalisation of women.

And it is not only in Israel-Palestine that women are crossing bridges and taking initiatives for peace. In Syria, amidst the devastating conflict that still rages on, women are active in many ways building striving to build peace and democracy. For example, they organise non-violent protests, being among the first to take to the streets in March 2011. Though it has become increasingly dangerous, many have continued these efforts. One example of this is the young women in Qamishli who campaigned for disarmament, hanging posters throughout the city and organizing support via Facebook. Women are also to the fore in distributing and monitoring humanitarian aid: because they are seen as less threatening, they are often able to transport needed supplies through checkpoints without being searched. An activist who attended one of Inclusive Security's workshops last year, for example, lived sixty kilometers from Aleppo and commuted each day to work; when her hometown was shelled, she smuggled medical supplies from Aleppo in her bags. Women also establish safe spaces for other women and children, and some have even created art therapy and other programs for psychological healing for citizens of all ages. For instance, through her *Foundation to Restore Education and Equality* in Syria, Rafif Jouejati, a member of the *Women Waging Peace Network*, as set up "Jasmine Tents", safe areas for women inside the country to recover from trauma and learn new job skills.[36] Women are also active in documenting human rights violations.

In addition to her work with the Local Coordination Committees (LCCs) of Syria, attorney and activist Razan Zeitouneh founded the *Violation Documentation Center* to monitor and report on kidnappings, detentions, disappearances, and murders by armed individuals in Syria.[37] Zeitouneh's courageous stance brought government opposition, and she was forced into hiding near Damascus for much of last year, ending with her being kidnapped on 9 December 2013. Her team was one of the first to report on the chemical weapons attack last August (2013). Women have also been successful in securing local-level ceasefires and release of prisoners.

In April 2011, 2,000 women and children blocked a highway in Banias and successfully demanded that hundreds of men who had been rounded up in neighbouring villages be released by the government.[38] Since that early protest, women have been leaders on this issue. Women have also negotiated the cessation of hostilities between armed actors on the local level in order to allow aid to pass through these zones. In Zabadani, a suburb of Damascus, a group of women pressured the local military council to accept a twenty-day ceasefire with regime forces.

Rather than wait for a democratic transition at the national level, Syrian women are busy promoting local and municipal elections. Since the country has experienced dictatorship for forty years, one woman in a town near Idlib is raising awareness of what free and fair elections entail.[39] She works with citizens and candidates to explain the electoral process, curtail corruption, and ensure voters know their rights and responsibilities. In Aleppo, female activists also lobbied for women to be guaranteed at least 25 per cent representation in the preparatory committee for local and provincial councils, half of the nominations for candidates, and 25 per cent of the seats in the final election. Women are also raising awareness about civil peace: to counteract the prevalent narratives of extremism and sectarianism, women have utilized different platforms to disseminate a message of peace and reconciliation. For example, in Qamishli, students held festivals to promote peace and coexistence between Arabs and Kurds. *Women Waging Peace Network* member Honey Al Sayed founded Radio SouriaLi, which broadcasts on the internet to bypass censors and reach Syrians inside and outside the country. The organization promotes civic engagement, community development, and responsible citizenship under the motto "Unity in Diversity".

Nor are women failing to develop plans for a future democratic and pluralistic state: *The Day After Project*, vice-chaired by Afra Jalabi (a member of *Women Waging Peace Network*), convened a series of meetings to outline a plan to reconstruct Syria and establish democracy once the country transitions out of conflict. They published a report with recommendations for reforming the security sector, drafting a new constitution, establishing transitional justice mechanisms, setting up free and fair elections, promoting the rule of law, and rebuilding the country's infrastructure.[40]

Inside Syria, small groups have gathered to lay out similar roadmaps. Currently, eight women are participating on the opposition's negotiating and technical teams, while two women are on the regime's delegation in the Geneva II peace talks.[41]

The female delegates at Geneva are in charge of important portfolios like negotiating prisoner release and humanitarian access to Homs. Finally, women are gathering in parallel to the negotiations to demand broader inclusion: forty-seven prominent women leaders gathered in Geneva in mid-January 2014 to develop and present recommendations to UN Special Envoy Lakhdar Brahimi. In addition to calling for an immediate ceasefire and humanitarian access, they asked that women make up at least 30 per cent of all negotiating teams and demanded a new constitution that guarantees equal citizenship to all Syrian people.[42]

Similarly, the *Syrian Women's Forum for Peac*e brought together a diverse group of sixty women in Damascus to develop a Syrian Women's Charter for Peace. It too goes beyond a cessation of hostilities to call for safe refugee return, human rights protections, and constitutional reform.[43]

Spirit, beauty, and vision

How can such initiatives, whether referring to embroidery as pride in identity, caring for children, or protesting outside a prison possibly be called the work of the Holy Spirit? Here I want to recall the connections I made initially: the Spirit in affliction evokes moral beauty through imagination and in vision.

Women refuse to split the public from the personal world, seeing this split as artificial. They refuse to accept the status quo as inevitable. Imagination and vision are integrally connected in working for peace with justice, but never separated from the homely and the ordinary. As Adrienne Rich wrote with such inspiration:

> Vision begins to happen in such a life
> as if a woman quietly walked away
> from the argument and jargon in a room
> and sitting down in the kitchen, began turning in her lap
> bits of yarn, calico and velvet scraps,
> laying them out absently on the scrubbed boards
> in the lamplight, with small rainbow-coloured shells
> sent in cotton-wool from somewhere far away,
> and skeins of milkweed from the nearest meadow— . . .
> Such a composition has nothing to do with eternity;

the striving for greatness, brilliance—
only with the musing of a mind
one with her body . . .
pulling the tenets together
with no mere will to mastery,
only care for the many-lived, unending
forms in which she finds herself [44]

Affliction and oppression are the context, but the same Spirit that drove the early missionaries from Jerusalem to Gaza, Syria, Egypt, and Macedon is inspiring and encouraging suffering communities in the Middle East not to give way to despair and to cherish the forms of beauty experienced in the great work for justice. But how did Paul experience this persecution towards the end of his life, when opposition mounted and affliction became the dominant factor of his missionary work? To this, in the final chapter, we now turn.

Notes

1. Euripides, *Medea*, Rex Warner (trans.) (Chicago: University of Chicago Press, 1970), lines 410–420.
2. George Eliot, *Impressions of Theophrastus Such* (London and Edinburgh: William Blackwood and Sons, 1879). Available at <http://www.gutenberg.org/ebooks/10762>.
3. *Letter to the Philippians.*
4. We know this from the Book of Revelation 2.18–29, where St John writes to the seven early Churches of Asia.
5. William Wordsworth, "Nutting", in Stephen Gill (ed.), *William Wordsworth* (Oxford: Oxford University Press, 1984), pp. 153–154.
6. Gerard Manley Hopkins, "God's Grandeur", in *Hopkins: Selected Poetry* (Oxford: Oxford University Press, 1996), p. 114.
7. Patrick Sherry, *Spirit and Beauty: an Introduction to Theological Aesthetics* (London: SCM, 1992, reprinted 2002), p. 69.

8. Ibid., p. 4.
9. Patrick Sherry develops a particular Trinitarian approach, developed by the Cappadocian Fathers and by more modern Russian interpreters like Paul Evdokimov. See Sherry, *Spirit and Beauty*, pp. 82–90. I do not mean in any way to undermine the sheer illuminating power of art but to develop a more inclusive approach to culture.
10. Ibid., p. 103.
11. John McIntyre, *Faith, Theology and Imagination*, (Edinburgh, 1987), p. 64.
12. Sherry, *Spirit and Beauty*, p. 113.
13. Victorin-Vangerud, *The Raging Hearth*, pp. 187–212.
14. Kyriocentric means "the rule of the Lord"—the phrase was invented by the renowned US feminist scripture scholar, Elisabeth Schüssler Fiorenza.
15. Victorin-Vangerud, *The Raging Hearth*, p. 187.
16. See Taylor, *The Go-Between God*, pp. 91–128.
17. Grey, *The Wisdom of Fools?*, p. 62.
18. Adrienne Rich, "For Memory", in *The Fact of a Doorframe: Selected Poems 1950–2001* (New York: W. & W. Norton, 2002), p. 174. Copyright © 2002, 1981 by Adrienne Rich. Used by permission of W. W. Norton & Company, Inc.
19. So writes Rosemary Sayigh, *Palestinians: From Peasants to Revolutionaries* (London: Zed Books, 2007) (Kindle edition). But Fatma Kassem speaks of women's stories told in the kitchen rather than the public living room; see Fatma Kassem, *Palestinian Women: Narrative Histories and Gendered Memory*, (London: Zed Books, 2011), p. 26.
20. Anbara Salam Khalidi, *Memoirs of an Early Arab Feminist: the Life and Activism of Anbara Salam Khalidi*, Tarif Khalidi (trans.) (London: Pluto Press, 2013), p. 142.
21. The *Sumud* Story House is an initiative of the *Arab Education Institute*. See <http://www.aeicenter.org>.
22. *Let me Tell you My Story: Women's Rights Stories from Four Communities in the Bethlehem District* (Bethlehem: Arab Educational Institute, 2013), p. 45.
23. Adrienne Rich, "The Desert as Garden of Paradise" in *The Fact of a Doorframe: Selected Poems 1950–2001* (New York: W. & W. Norton, 2002), p. 222. Copyright © 2002, 1989 by Adrienne Rich. Used by permission of W. W. Norton & Company, Inc.

24. Adrienne Rich, "Cartographies of Silence", in *The Fact of a Doorframe: Selected Poems 1950–2001* (New York: W. & W. Norton, 2002), p. 139–140. Copyright © 2002 by Adrienne Rich. Used by permission of W. W. Norton & Company, Inc.
25. Kassem, *Palestinian Women*, p. 111. But see also pp. 91–128 for a fuller explanation.
26. George Eliot, *Middlemarch* (Hertfordshire: Wordsworth Classics, 1994), p. 162.
27. I hope the reader will bear with me as to the problem of the lack of historical evidence we have for Lydia and accept her being imagined here as a symbolic matrix.
28. Kassem *Palestinian Women*, p. 115.
29. Khalidi, *Memoirs of an Early Arab Feminist*, p. 143.
30. Khader Musleh, "Palestinian Embroidery and Textiles: a Nation's Tale", in *This Week in Palestine* (6 December 2006).
31. See Mazin Qumsiyeh, *Popular Resistance in Palestine: a History of Hope and Empowerment* (London: Pluto Press, 2011), p. 234.
32. Gila Svirsky, "A Peace Movement of her own," in Maurine and Robert Tobin (eds.), *How Long O Lord? Christian, Jewish and Muslim Voices from the Ground and Visions for the Future* (Cambridge Mass.: Cowley Publications, 2002), pp. 163–170; citation at p. 164.
33. Ibid., p.165.
34. The names of the individual groups are, in addition to *Women in Black*, *Bat Shalom* (an Israeli-Palestinian partnership of women for peace); The Fifth Mother (the re-grouped Four Mothers movement which plays a major role in bringing to an end to the Israeli occupation of Lebanon); Machsom Watch (a group that monitors checkpoints); NELED (an organization of "Women for Coexistence"); Noga Feminist Journal; New Profile (a feminist movement for the de-militarisation of Israel); WILPF (the Israeli Chapter of the Women's International League for Peace and Freedom); and TAND (the Movement of Democratic Women for Israel). These consist primarily of Palestinian citizens of Israel seeking equality for an empowerment of women.
35. Svirsky, pp. 166–167. See this article for a full list of principles.
36. <http://www.free-syria-foundation.org/the-jasmine-tent.html>.
37. Her findings are available at <http://www.vdc-sy.info/index.php/en/home>.

38. Kristin Williams "10 ways Syrian Women are building peace and democracy", Institute for Inclusive Security (21 February 2014), at <http://www.inclusivesecurity.org/10-ways-syrian-women-building-peace-democracy/>. Since that early protest, women have been leaders on this issue; for example, Rima Fleihan is in charge of negotiating it for the opposition in Geneva. Syrian activist Kefah ali Deeb has said, "The case of the detainees—our families and friends and neighbors who are detained—is more important than all political cards". Kristin Williams is a Writer and Program Associate at The Institute for Inclusive Security, where she works to strengthen women's leadership in the Middle East and North Africa, and makes the case globally for women's substantive participation in the peace and security decisions that affect their lives.
39. The events described in this paragraph are taken from Williams, "10 ways"; the anonymity of the women is a reflection of the article in question.
40. *The Day After: supporting a Democratic Transition in Syria* (Syria: The Day After, 2012); available for download from <http://thedayafter-sy.org>.
41. "In the lead-up to the Geneva II negotiations, Syrian activists, local and international organizations, the UN, and various foreign governments made a clear demand: **Women must be at the table**. During the first round of talks in late January, both the regime and opposition delegations heeded that call, to differing extents. Below, we've documented what we know so far about women's formal roles in the Syria peace talks.This is a promising step forward, but we still say: **More women must be meaningfully involved in the negotiations.** To ensure women's unique perspectives and needs are a core part of the discussions, all of the parties—including the UN in their role as mediator—must ensure representatives of diverse constituencies from inside Syria are consulted and engaged throughout the entire process. (We've written extensively about models for doing so.)"; Williams, "10 ways".
42. Ibid.
43. Ibid.
44. Adrienne Rich, "Transcendental Etude", in *The Dream of a Common Language: Poems 1974–1977* (New York: W. & W. Norton, 1980), pp. 76–77. Copyright © 1978 by W. W. Norton & Company, Inc. Used by permission of W. W. Norton & Company, Inc.

CHAPTER 7

From old Jaffa to Caesarea—the Spirit leads into the future!

We all face today a way that is blocked and a future that promises only woe. Our word to all our Christian brothers and sisters is a word of hope, patience, steadfastness and new action for a better future.

Kairos Palestine[1]

We live today within a diverse and interdependent world household. Yet as beautiful and profound as our world can be, from within this house emerge the groans of fear, unrecognised loss, and suffering. Dignity, as the blessing of God the Spirit, provides a pneumatological concept with connections to social movements within and beyond the Christian Churches that struggle for justice in our shared household.

***Nancy Victorin-Vangerud,* The Raging Hearth**[2]

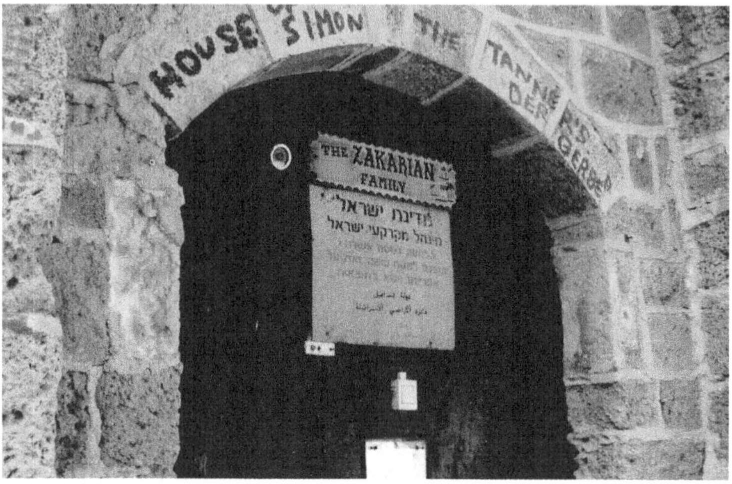

Figure 5: House of Simon the Tanner, Old Jaffa.

I have come on my own journey to where the story of this book began: to the (presumed) house of Simon the Tanner in Old Jaffa, once the biblical town of Joppa, where Peter received the decisive revelation of the Gentile Pentecost (Acts 10). This, as we have been witnessing, changed the whole understanding of his own mission and that of the fledgling Christian community.

Jaffa—one of the oldest functioning harbours in the world, and thirty miles south of Caesarea—was the main port of the coast before the Israelis constructed the ports of Haifa and Ashdod.[3] With a population today of about 60,000, Jaffa has a Jewish majority (mostly from other Middle-Eastern and North African countries) with a sizeable Arab Christian and Muslim population. I had come from the modern, thriving Israeli city of Tel Aviv, founded on the outskirts of Jaffa in 1909, and now encompassing this more ancient city.[4] Walking around the bustling shopping malls in the centre of Tel Aviv, it seemed to me to be another world. It was as if the worsening sufferings of the Palestinians in the West Bank and Gaza had been rendered invisible.

Historically, the name Joppa appears for the first time in the list of cities that Thutmose III captured in fifteenth century BC. The Greek legend of Andromeda—being bound to a rock and then rescued by Theseus—was first associated with Joppa by the Roman historian Strabo (first century

AD), and Andromeda's rock lies in a dramatic position in the old harbour. Today, Jaffa's harbour holds only small fishing boats, but it is inspiring to recall that this was the port to which Jonah came when fleeing from the Lord to Tarshish (Jonah 1.3). Also, that for the construction of Solomon's Temple, cedars were floated from Phoenicia to Joppa and then transported to Jerusalem (2 Chronicles 2.16). Its significance during the Ottoman Empire was as the main port of entry to the Holy Land: here would journey countless pilgrims and visitors.

Figure 6: The port of Old Jaffa today.

Our story began with Peter who journeyed to Joppa, soon after the conversion of Paul, from nearby Lydda, because a devoted disciple, Tabitha (Dorcas), had just died (Acts 9.36). Peter prayed over her, and then told her to get up and live again. This was the most dramatic of his miracles and the most influential in encouraging conversion in Jaffa. All the while he was staying in the house of Simon the Tanner, on whose rooftop he received the revelation of the Spirit as described in Chapter 2.

Here the Holy Spirit led the early Christians to a deeper understanding of the universality of the Jesus movement and eventually led Peter himself to Rome. But the joy of these revelatory beginnings is now clouded by the reality that confronts Christianity in the Middle East, as we have been exploring. Before facing the challenge today, we return to Paul and his last difficult days in Palestine.

Last days of the great missionary in the Holy Land

I reluctantly turned my steps northwards, from imagining Peter's revelation on the rooftop in the old port of Jaffa, to Caesarea, a port mid-way between Tel Aviv and Haifa, on the Israeli coastal plain near the city of Hadera. Modern Caesarea has a population of 4,500 people. It is the only Israeli locality managed by a private organization, the Caesarea Development Corporation, and also one of the most populous localities not recognized as a local council.[5]

What I sought and found was not the modern Caesarea, but rather the old city, now an Israeli National park. This ancient town was built by Herod the Great (around 25–13 BC) as the port city of *Caesarea Maritima*. It provided an administrative centre for Judaea, a province of the Roman Empire, and later the capital of the Byzantine province of *Palaestina Prima*. Following the Muslim conquest in the seventh century, the city had an Arab majority until the Crusader renovation, but was abandoned after the conquest of the Mamluks.[6]

What I saw were the ruins of Herod's palace where Paul was a prisoner for two years. The Biblical scholar Jerome Murphy-O'Connor has described how the way the life of Paul—as Luke understands it—is shown to mirror the life of Jesus in many ways.[7] At this point, Paul's experience of trial and imprisonment also reflects the trial of Jesus before both Jewish and Roman authorities. Paul first stood trial before High Priest Ananias, and again before the procurator, Felix, in Jerusalem; he was moved to Caesarea and tried before the governor, Festus, and eventually by King Agrippa at his insistence that he be tried as a Roman citizen.[8] Just as Jesus in his trial was sent by Pontius Pilate to Herod Antipas, so too Paul is sent by the procurator Festus to the Jewish king Agrippa.

In Paul's extended *apologia* before the King, we hear again the story of his transformative Damascus experience (Acts 26.12–18). Once more, he insists—as he has done consistently—that the purpose of the Messiah was to proclaim light unto both Jews and Gentiles (Acts 26.23). Now the stage is set for Luke's final drama: in Jesus' case, when Pilate appealed to the crowd, believing in Jesus' innocence, the cry was "crucify him" (John 19.6). In Paul's case, the decision was to send him to the Emperor in Rome. There the final act would unfold.[9]

Opinions vary as to the extent of Paul's activity at and travels from Rome. If we believe in the authenticity of the Second Letter to Timothy, Paul was very isolated in Rome at the end of his life, his only companion being the faithful Luke (2 Timothy 4.9). This would present another comparison with the forsakenness of Jesus at his death and Paul's continual experience of affliction.

Figure 7: The ruins of Herod's palace, Caesarea.

Figure 8: The Old Port, Caesarea.

But now, as I look from the ruins of Herod's palace, to the port from where Paul would sail, only to experience the shipwreck and miraculous escape that Luke relates (Acts 27.1–44), my focus is not so much on the abiding power of the Spirit with Paul in his last days, but more on where the power of the Spirit is active now with the Christians who remain in the Holy Lands and the Middle East.

Despite the new revelations of the Spirit experienced through the power of mutuality, connectedness, steadfastness (*sumud*), beauty, imagination, and bridge-building into the unknown that we have been following (amidst other themes), there is a desperate sense of impasse today in many Middle Eastern countries. Christians cry out, "How long must we continue to endure conflict and violence?" How can the Holy Spirit come to their aid in ever-worsening circumstances and enduring affliction?

In conclusion, I look two ways. First, I recall the striking words of the Jesuit priest, Fr. Peter de Brul, at the Sabeel Conference in Jerusalem, November 2013.[10] He drew us to the special place of the mystical when he spoke of God as completion, or the experience of the completeness of God, of the fullness of God, but also of God's absence. In this, the "dark night" of the Palestinian people, I suggest that the way of mysticism offers sustaining resources in a time of affliction. I perceive already that there is a mystical turn to God, or mystical experience of the presence of God, similar to that of St John of the Cross in his *Dark Night of the Soul,* written from a Spanish prison at the time of the Inquisition.[11] From Britain, a similar sense can be seen in the work of the anchoress Julian of Norwich, who wrote down her visions just after the collective despair of the Black Death in the fourteenth century, when a third of the clergy in Europe were wiped out.[12] Karl Rahner's prophetic words written in 1966 also come to mind (translation is mine):

> Der Fromme von Morgen wird ein "Mystiker" sein, einer, der etwas "erfahren" hat, oder er nicht mehr sein . . .[13]
>
> *The believer of tomorrow will be a mystic, a person who experiences something, or he/she will cease to exist . . .*

Mystics from many historical contexts speak to our desolation with a deepening hope of light and the intensity of God's love in and through the dark night. Mystical love for God, wrote the late Dorothee Soelle, a German liberation theologian, "Makes us open to God's absence: the senseless, spiritless suffering that separates humans from all that makes for life".[14] For Soelle, the only place to find God was in the political struggle. She had discovered this painfully at a demonstration in Bonn in 1983 when the police turned water cannons against those protesting against the US nuclear weapons stationed in Germany. Somehow she had to find the courage to speak to the bedraggled protesters and she found herself screaming to God—"Why have you forsaken us?" But then she found the answer coming from deep within:

> The God to whom this prayer was addressed was as grieved as we were, small like us, with no bank account or bombs in the background . . . And yet God was with us that night.[15]

Very early on in her search she visited the Jewish philosopher Martin Buber in Jerusalem. On her telling him that she was a theologian, he surprised her by replying, "Theo-logy—how do you do that? There is no *logos* of God".[16] This disconcerting answer prompted her life-long exploration in poetry and myth, culminating in what would be recognised as a full-blown mystical theology. Her last book, *The Silent Cry: Mysticism and Resistance,* is her most explicit expression of this yearning for God that fuels resistance to injustice and, eluding complete rational expression, is a theme common to many faiths. *The Silent Cry* pulled together the two strands that inspired her life: God and Justice. Written when she emerged out of a coma from which few thought she would survive, all her familiar themes are brought together—nature, suffering, community, politics, relation, justice, joy, *eros*—all finding meaning in the yearning for God, a God sought in a diversity of traditions.

But how does Soelle's mystical journey help the present crisis of Middle Eastern Christians? It is the way that she links the spiritual journey of faith with the struggle of resistance:

She does not accept mysticism as an "inward" journey taken by and on behalf of the self. The mystical journey "leads into a healing that is at the same time resistance".[17]

What mystics give struggling Christians today is a pedagogy of hope. Julian of Norwich wants that we should be rooted in God's love, in the experience of "Love is his meaning",[18] knowing that, through Christ, the entire Trinity is drawing us deeper into saving grace, as we trust that Christ has done everything for our redemption. But that does not mean that God has abandoned the violence and affliction of the present world. Julian stresses that it is the sense of the absence of God that gives pain. A pedagogy of hope draws us into the conviction that there is *no space that the mercy and redemptive grace of God cannot reach.*

But the second direction to pursue is the urgent call from the Middle East to Christians of the West. Just as Paul responded to the cry, "Come over to Macedon and help us!" (Acts 16.9), so too must modern Christians turn to aid those in the land which gave rise to their faith. Just as the early Christian disciples responded to the needs of fledgling communities across the Mediterranean, becoming faithful witnesses and enduring martyrdom for the faith, so too do we see this happening today across many countries of the Middle East (as this book has been exploring), such that many are again facing death, often directly because of the faith (this has happened again recently in Syria: the Jesuit priest Fr Van der Lugt was killed in Homs in April 2013).[19]

Again, Eastern Christians are calling out for an active solidarity. During the Easter celebrations of 2014, His Beatitude Gregorios III, Patriarch of Antioch, left us in no doubt in his Paschal letter with his appeal to us on behalf of the most weak and vulnerable of his country:

> On the basis of our Christian faith and spiritual mission and role as pastor and Patriarch, we turn to everyone: the President of our country and his colleagues, all Arab countries, the United States of America, the Russian Federation, countries of the European Union, all nations of the world, pacifists, Nobel Peace Prize-winners, all men and women of good will, the pure-hearted, leaders of social media, people of letters, thinkers, captains of industry and commerce, arms merchants . . . and call upon you all to expend every possible effort for peace in Syria. The Syrian tragedy has exceeded every measure and limit! It has adversely affected nearly every Syrian citizen. We ask God to hear this appeal. May he guide your hearts to heed this appeal from him and from us.[20]

He continued in his heart-rending appeal:

> Death reigns in Syria! We cannot continue the death march! We must summon up our efforts, at home and abroad, government, opposition, all parties, and persons of good will, to staunch the flow of Syrian blood and walk towards resurrection! We are all sons and daughters of Syria, to whom has been given the light of life. We are called to life, not death. As a Syrian citizen and Syrian patriarch, I beseech every Syrian to walk, with his fellow-citizens, on the road of resurrection and life, that they all might have life and that they might have it more abundantly (cf. John 10.10). No more war! No more violence! No more massacres![21]

His words, with explicit reference to Syria, also apply with burning relevance to Gaza, Egypt, and Palestine, and the Spirit's presence among Middle Eastern Christians. As he says:

> Syria is the land of the Resurrection. At the gates of Damascus, Paul of Tarsus saw Christ risen from the dead. He came to Damascus as a persecutor. He left it as an apostle and preacher of the Resurrection. That is why Syria is the land of the Resurrection. As we said: the title of its children is "Children of the Resurrection."[22]

This appeal to the global community is also an explicit summons in the document of the Christian Churches of Palestine, *Kairos Palestine: A Moment of Truth*. Here an appeal is made specifically to the international community:

> Our word to the international community is to stop the principle of double standards and insist on the international resolutions regarding the Palestinian problem with regard to all parties.[23]

A British response to this focused specifically on a call to action.[24] It emphasized "Go and see!", a call to visit the holy places and understand the situation of Palestinian Christians. It called for political action in terms of the Boycott, Divestment, and Sanction campaign (BDS),[25] for a challenge to the misuse of the Bible in support of Zionist misinterpretations, for prayer, but, most of all, for a clear choice for justice and an end to silence. It is a call that must be answered by all who are concerned not only for Christians but for all people who are living in affliction yet who never cease to hope.

From the power of the Spirit, from the first beginnings of Christianity to the steady presence of the Spirit in the contemporary times of affliction, God's promise is unflinching (John 14:26):

> The Holy Spirit will teach you everything and remind you all I have said to you.

But in the same breath, Jesus promises that (John 14.27):

> Peace I leave with you, my peace I give you.

How we answer that urgent call may be the test of the very integrity of being Christian today.

Notes

1. *A Moment of Truth: A word of faith, hope, and love from the heart of Palestinian suffering* (Jerusalem: Kairos, 2009), p. 13.
2. Nancy Victorin-Vangerud, *The Raging Hearth*, p. 211.
3. <http://www.bibleplaces.com/joppa.htm>.
4. Tel Aviv means "the Hill of Spring", and it is the same name as the city of a settlement in Babylon during the Exile (Ezekiel 3.15). Today, the Tel Aviv area is the largest metropolitan area in Israel.
5. <http://en.wikipedia.org/wiki/Caesarea>.
6. The Mamluks were a military caste in medieval Egypt that rose from the ranks of slaves. This warrior class lasted from the ninth to the nineteenth centuries AD, powerful in various Muslim societies, especially in Egypt, but also in the Levant, Mesopotamia, and India. In some cases, they attained the rank of sultan. Most notably, Mamluk factions seized the sultanate for themselves in Egypt and Syria in a period known as the Mamluk Sultanate (1250–1517).
7. Jerome Murphy-O'Connor, *Jesus and Paul—Parallel Lives* (Minnesota, Collegeville: Michael Glazier Liturgical Press, 2007).
8. Agrippa is in fact Herod Agrippa II, the fourth Herod to appear in Luke's work: "Herod the Great, the famous builder of Caesarea and Masada and spectacular renovator of the second temple, reigned at the time of the infancies of John the Baptist and Jesus (Luke 1.5). Herod the Tetrarch (Antipas), son of Herod the Great, ruled Galilee and Perea during the rest of Jesus' life. Herod Agrippa (ruled AD 41–44), grandson of Herod the Great, appeared (and died) in Acts 12. Now we meet the great grandson,

Herod Agrippa II (who ruled after AD 50)"; see Murphy-O'Connor, *Jesus and Paul*, p. 110.

9. We know that Paul arrived in Rome c. 60 and spent another two years under house arrest (beyond his two years in prison in Caesarea): see Acts 28.16.
10. This celebrated 25 years of the work of Sabeel in Israel, Palestine, and internationally.
11. St John of the Cross, *The Dark Night*, in Kieran Kavanaugh OCD (ed.), *Selected Writings* (London: SPCK, 1987), pp. 157–209.
12. Julian of Norwich, *The Revelations of Divine Love*, James Walsh SJ (trans.) (Wheathampstead: Anthony Clarke Books, 1973).
13. Karl Rahner, "Frőmmigkeit Frűher und Heute", in *Schriften zur Theologie*, VII, (Einsiedeln/Zurich/Koln: Verlaganstalt Benziger and Co., 1966), pp. 11–31, at p. 22.
14. Dorothee Soelle, *The Silent Cry: Mysticism and Resistance*, Barbara and Martin Rumscheidt (trans.) (Minneapolis: Fortress, 2001), p. 140.
15. Dorothee Soelle, "Liberating our God-Talk: From Authoritarian Otherness to Mystical Inwardness", in Ursula King (ed.), *Liberating Women: New Theological Directions* (Bristol: University of Bristol Press, 1991), pp. 40–52, at p. 46.
16. Dorothee Soelle, "Breaking the Ice of the Soul: Theology and Literature in Search of a New Language," in Sarah A. Pinnock (ed.), *The Theology of Dorothee Soelle* (London/New York: Trinity Press International, 2003), pp. 31–53; citation at p. 31.
17. Carter Heyward, "Crossing Over: Dorothee Soelle and the Transcendence of God", in Pinnock (ed.), *The Theology of Dorothee Soelle* (London: Bloomsbury, 2003), pp. 221–238; citation at p. 235.
18. Julian of Norwich, *The Revelations of Divine Love*, p. 209.
19. "Syria: Dutch priest Fr van der Lugt shot dead in Homs", BBC News (7 April 2014), <http://www.bbc.com/news/world-middle-east-26927068>; and Peter Jesserer Smith, "Jesuit priest saw Christ crucified again in Syrian", *National Catholic Register* (15 April, 2014), <http://www.ncregister.com/daily-news/jesuit-priest-saw-christ-crucified-again-in-syria>.
20. Paschal Letter (20 April 2014) of His Beatitude Gregorios III, Patriarch of Antioch and All the East, of Alexandria and of Jerusalem, p. 7.
21. Ibid., p. 7.

22. Ibid., p. 12.
23. *A Moment of Truth*, p. 25.
24. *Time for Action: A British Response to* A Moment of Truth, *the Kairos Palestine Document* (August 2013); document available at <http://www.kairosbritain.org.uk>.
25. Ibid., pp. 23–25.

Bibliography

Politics, Biography, History and Geography

Abu Sarah, Aziz, 'First person: five things I learned in Syrian refugee camps', *National Geographic* (19 September 2013), <http://news.nationalgeographic.com/news/2013/09/130920-syria-refugees-camps-war-children/>.

Abuelaish, Izzeldin, *I Shall Not Hate: A Gaza Doctor's Journey on the Road to Peace and Human Dignity* (London: Bloomsbury, 2011).

Brown, Peter, 'The Rise and Function of the Holy Man in Late Antiquity', *Journal of Roman Studies*, vol. 61 (1971), pp. 80-100.

Carter, Terry, Dunston, Lara, and Thomas, Amelia, *Syria and Lebanon* (London: Lonely Planet, 2008).

Chacour, Elias, and Jensen, Mary, *We belong to the Land* (Indiana: University of Notre Dame Press, 2001).

Chacour, Elias, and Hazard, David, *Blood Brothers* (New Jersey: Chosen Books, 1984).

Chomsky, Noam, 'My Visit to Gaza, the World's Largest Open-Air Prison', *Truth-Out* (4 November 2012), <http://www.chomsky.info/articles/20121104.htm>.

Cook, Catherine, Hanien, Adam, and Kay, Adam, *Stolen Youth: the Politics of Israel's Detention of Palestinian Children* (London: Pluto Press 2004).

Dalrymple, William, *From the Holy Mountain: A Journey in the Shadow of Byzantium* (London: Harper-Collins, 1997).

Danahar, Paul, *The New Middle East: The World After the Arab Spring* (London: Bloomsbury 2013).

Eliot, George, *Middlemarch* (Hertfordshire: Wordsworth Classics, 1994).

Eliot, George, *Impressions of Theophrastus Such* (London and Edinburgh: William Blackwood and Sons, 1979).

Eliot, T. S., *Collected Poems 1909-1962* (London: Faber and Faber, 1974).

Euripides, *Medea*, Warner, Rex (trans.), (Chicago: University of Chicago Press, 1970).

Falk, Richard, 'The Latest Gaza Catastrophe: Will They Ever Learn?', from his blog *Global Justice in the 21st Century* (20 November 2013), <http://richardfalk.wordpress.com/2012/11/18/the-latest-gaza-catastrophe-will-they-ever-learn/>.

Falk, Richard, 'The latest Gaza catastrophe', Aljazeera (18 November 2012), <http://www.aljazeera.com/indepth/opinion/2012/11/2012111874429224963.html>.

Frymann, Abigail, 'Egyptian bishop voices hopes for new constitution', in *The Tablet* (21 December 2013).

Gaillard, Philippe. 'Memory never forgets Miracles', in Rittner, Carol, *et al* (eds.), *Genocide in Rwanda: Complicity of the Churches*, (St Paul, MN: Paragon House, 2004), pp.111-116

Gill, Stephen (ed.), *William Wordsworth* (Oxford: Oxford University Press, 1984).

Greaves, Mark, 'The City I love is in ruins', *The Catholic Herald* (18 October 2012).

Griffith, Stephen, 'Nostalgia for the regime of Assad', in *The Church Times* (25 October 2013), p. 15.

Hass, Amira, *Drinking the Sea at Gaza: Days and Nights in a Land under Siege*, Wesley, Elana, and Kaufman-Lacusta, Maxine (trans.) (New York: Holt paperback, 1996).

Hass, Amira, 'Otherwise Occupied/Labour is concerned', *Ha'aretz* (13 December 2010).

Hill, Evan, 'Egypt's Christians under Attack', Aljazeera America (21 August, 2013), <http://america.aljazeera.com/articles/2013/8/21/egypt-s-christiansunderattack.html>.

Hokayem, Emile *Uprising and the Fracturing of the Levant* (Abingdon: Routledge, 2013).

Hopkins, Gerard Manley, *Selected Poetry* (Oxford: Oxford University Press, 1996).

Howerton, Jason, 'President Obama: I am 'deeply concerned' by the military takeover in Egypt', *The Blaze* (3 July 2013), <http://www.theblaze.com/stories/2013/07/03/president-obama-i-am-deeply-concerned-by-the-military-takeover-in-egypt>.

Jeffrey, Paul, 'Gaza church nurtures hope despite Israeli blockade and Hamas control', Catholic News Service (22 February 2011), <http://www.catholicnews.com/data/stories/cns/1100730.htm>.

Jenkins, Simon, 'The Red Cross needs to Reclaim its hi-jacked Neutrality', *The Guardian* (1 November 2013).

Jones, Owen, 'Libya is a disaster we helped create: we cannot stay silent', in *The Guardian* (24 March 2014), p. 29.

Kamil, Jill, *Christianity in the Land of the Pharaohs: The Coptic Orthodox Church* (Cairo: The American University in Cairo Press, 2002).

Kassem, Fatma, *Palestinian Women: Narrative Histories and Gendered Memory* (London: Zed Books, 2011).

Khader Musleh, 'Palestinian Embroidery and Textiles: a Nation's Tale', in *This Week in Palestine* (6 December 2006).

Khalidi, Anbara Salam, *Memoirs of an Early Arab Feminist: the Life and Activism of Anbara Salam Khalidi,* Khalidi, Tarif (trans.) (Beirut, 1978; reprinted, London: Pluto Press, 2013).

Kingsley, Patrick and Chulov, Martin, 'Mohamed Morsi ousted in Egypt's second revolution in two years', *The Guardian* (3 July 2013), <http://www.theguardian.com/world/2013/jul/03/mohamed-morsi-egypt-second-revolution>.

Kirkpatrick, David D., and Fahim, Karen, 'Attack on Christians in Egypt Comes After a Pledge', *The New York Times* (8 April 2013).

Let me Tell you My Story: Women's Rights stories from Four Communities in the Bethlehem District (Bethlehem: Arab Educational Institute, 2013).

Levy, Gideon, The Punishment of Gaza (London: Verso, 2010).

McClure, Ian, 'A cure for the disease of hate' in BMJ (14 September 2011); <http://www.bmj.com/content/343/bmj.d5715>.

McLellan, David, *Simone Weil: Utopian Pessimist* (Oxford: Palgrave Macmillan, 1989).

Meinardus, Otto F.A., *Two Thousand Years of Coptic Christianity* (Cairo: The American University in Cairo Press, 1999).

Meyer, Martin A., *History of the City of Gaza: From the Earliest Times to the Present Day* (New York: The Columbia University Press, 1907).

Moodey, Jeremy, Letter to the *Church Times* (24 January 2014), p. 6.

Moschos, John, *The Spiritual Meadow*, John Wortley (trans) (Kalamazoo; Cistercian Publications, 1992).

Mullen, Jethro, 'Number of Syrian refugees rises above 2 million, U.N. agency says', CNN (4 September 2014), <http://edition.cnn.com/2013/09/03/world/meast/syria-refugees-unhcr>.

Nassar, Nadim, 'Jihad and Geneva', Awareness Foundation (27 January 2014), <http://www.awareness-foundation.co.uk/index.php/nadim/102>.

Nassar, Nadim, 'Weapons don't Stop War', in *The Tablet* (22 June 2013), p. 6.

O'Neill, Zora (ed.), *Lonely Planet: Egypt* (London: Lonely Planet Publications, 2012).

Omer, Mohammad, 'Gaza's Christian Community – Serenity, Solidarity and Soulfulness', *The Washington Report on Middle Eastern Affairs* (January–February 2008), pp. 16-17.

Pappé, Ilan, *The Forgotten Palestinians: A History of the Palestinians in Israel* (Yale: Yale University Press, 2011).

Pappé, Ilan, *The Ethnic Cleansing of the Palestinians*, (Oxford: Oneworld, 2006).

Pinnock, Sarah A. (ed.), *The Theology of Dorothee Soelle* (London/New York: Trinity Press International, 2003).

Qumsiyeh, Mazin, *Popular Resistance in Palestine: a History of Hope and Empowerment* (London: Pluto Press, 2011).

Mitri Raheb, 'Culture as the art to Breathe', <http://www.annadwa.org/news/newsletter_sep06.htm>.

Mitri Raheb, 'Culture as the art of breathing', van Teeffelen (ed.), *Challenging the Wall*, pp. 16-19.

Rassam, Suha, *Christianity in Iraq* (Leominster: Gracewing, 2005, repr. 2010).

Rich, Adrienne, *Poems 1985-88* (New York: W. and W. Norton, 1989).

Rich, Adrienne, *A Wild Patience has taken me this Far: Poems 1978-1981* (New York: W. & W. Norton, 1981).

Rich, Adrienne, *The Dream of a Common Language* (New York: W. & W. Norton 1980).

Roy, Sara, *A Failing Peace: Gaza and the Israeli-Palestinian Conflict* (London: Pluto Press, 2007).

Sayigh, Rosemary, *Palestinians: From Peasants to Revolutionaries* (London: Zed Books, 2007).

Sedley, S., et al, *Children in Military Custody*, (June 2012), <http://www.childreninmilitarycustody.org>.

Siddique, Haroon 'Gaza crisis: Talks continue as Palestinian death toll approaches 700 – as it happened', *The Guardian* (23 July 2013), <http://www.theguardian.com/world/2014/jul/23/gaza-crisis-plo-supports-hamas-conditions-for-ceasefire-live-updates>.

Smith, Peter Jesserer, 'Jesuit priest saw Christ crucified again in Syrian', *National Catholic Register* (15 April 2014), <http://www.ncregister.com/daily-news/jesuit-priest-saw-christ-crucified-again-in-syria>.

Soueif, Ahdaf, *Cairo, My City, My Revolution* (London: Bloomsbury, 2012).

Sozomen, *History of the Church in Nine Books* (London: Samuel Bagster and Sons, 1846), 9 vols.

Svirsky, Gila, 'A Peace Movement of her own', in Tobin, Maurine and Robert (eds.), *How Long O Lord? Christian, Jewish and Muslim Voices from the Ground and Visions for the Future* (Cambridge Mass.: Cowley Publications, 2002), pp. 163-170.

Tadros, Mariam, 'Lebanon', from her blog *Nomad Heart* (24 April 2013).

Tornielli, Andrea, 'Christians are the Arab Spring's biggest losers, says Melkite archbishop Chacour', *Vatican Insider* (7 June 2013), <http://vaticaninsider.lastampa.it/en/world-news/detail/articolo/medio-oriente-middle-east-medio-oriente-25187/>.

Uncredited, 'Syria: Dutch priest Fr van der Lugt shot dead in Homs', BBC News (7 April 2014), <http://www.bbc.com/news/world-middle-east-26927068>.

Uncredited, 'Orthodox Bishop Decries Largest Massacre of Syrian Christians', *Zenit* (5 November 2013), <http://www.zenit.org/en/articles/orthodox-bishop-decries-largest-massacre-of-syrian-christians>.

Uncredited, 'One third of Syrian Christians have gone, says cleric', World Watch Monitor (23 October 2013), <https://www.worldwatchmonitor.org/2013/10/2763901/>.

Uncredited, 'Egypt: Pope Tawadros rebukes Morsi over Cathedral clash', BBC News (9 April 2013), <http://www.bbc.co.uk/news/world-middle-east-22083168>.

Uncredited, 'Alexandria church bomb: Egypt police on high alert', BBC News (3 January 2012), <http://www.bbc.co.uk/news/world-middle-east-12107084>.

van Teeffelen, Toine (ed.), *Challenging the Wall: toward a Pedagogy of Hope* (Bethlehem: Arab Education Centre, 2008).

van Teeffelen, and Giacaman, Fuad, 'Sumud: Resistance in Daily Life', in van Teeffelen (ed.), *Challenging the Wall*, pp. 20-34.

Victorin-Vangerud, Nancy M., *The Raging Hearth: Spirit in the Household of God* (Missouri: Chalice Press, 2000).

Vlazna, Vacy, 'Gaza calling: A Christmas appeal to Pope Francis', Aljazeera (23 December 2013), <http://www.aljazeera.com/indepth/opinion/2013/12/gaza-calling-christmas-appeal-pope-francis-201312221232347236.html>.

Williams, Kirsten, '10 ways Syrian Women are building peace and democracy', Institute for Inclusive Security (21 February 2014), <http://www.inclusivesecurity.org/10-ways-syrian-women-building-peace-democracy/>.

Scripture, Theology and Spirituality

Avakian, Sylvie, 'The Mystery of Divine Love in the Apophatic Theology of Bishop George Khodr', in *Theological Review*, 33 (2012), pp. 39-68.

Bailey, Kenneth, *Jesus through Middle Eastern Eyes* (London: SPCK 2008).

Bradley, Mike, 'Long Suffering – The 4th Fruit of the Holy Spirit', *Ezine Articles* (20 January 2008), <http://www.ezinearticles.com/?id=938887>.

Brock, Sebastian (ed. and trans.), *The Wisdom of Saint Isaac the Syrian* (Oxford: SLG Press, 1997).

Dick, Ignace, 'Christian Syria', in *Living Stones Year Book 2013: Christianity in the Middle East: Theology, History, Politics, and Dialogue* (London: Melisende 2013), pp. 70-83.

Evdokimov, Paul, *L'Orthodoxie* (Paris: Desclée de Brouwer, 1965).

Flannery, Austin (ed.), *Documents of the Second Vatican Council* (New York: Costello Publishing Company, 1975).

His Beatitude Gregorios III, Patriarch of Antioch and All the East, of Alexandria and of Jerusalem, *Paschal Letter* (20 April 2014).

Grey, Mary, *The Resurrection of Peace: A Gospel Journey to Easter and Beyond* (London: SPCK, 2012).

Grey, Mary, *The Advent of Peace: A Gospel Journey to Christmas* (London: SPCK, 2010).

Grey, Mary, 'Taking a Deep Breath: Spiritual Resources for a Pedagogy of Hope', in van Teeffelen (ed.), *Challenging the Wall*, pp. 9-15.

Grey, Mary, *The Wisdom of Fools? Seeking Revelation for Today* (London: SPCK, 1993).

Gutiérrez, Gustavo, *Los Casas: In search of the Poor of Jesus Christ* (New York, Maryknoll: Orbis, 1993).

Gutiérrez, Gustavo, 'How can God be discussed from the perspective of Ayacucho?', in *On the Threshold of the Third Millennium, Concilium* (1990/1) pp. 103-114.

Gutiérrez, Gustavo, *On Job: God-talk and the suffering of the Innocent* (New York, Maryknoll: Orbis, 1989).

Heyward, Carter, 'Crossing Over: Dorothee Soelle and the Transcendence of God', in Pinnock (ed.), *The Theology of Dorothee Soelle*, pp. 221-238.

Heyward, Carter, *Our Passion for Justice*, (Cleveland: The Pilgrim Press, 1984).

The Holy Bible, New Revised Standard Edition (London: Collins, 1989).

John of the Cross, *The Complete Works*, E. Alison Peers (ed. and trans.) (Westminster, MD: Newman Press 1953; reprinted Sheed and Ward, 1978).

John of the Cross, *The Dark Night*, in Kavanaugh, Kieran (ed.), *Selected Writings* (London: SPCK, 1987), pp. 157-209.

Julian of Norwich, *The Revelations of Divine Love*, Walsh, James (trans.) (Wheathampstead: Anthony Clarke books 1973).

Khoury, Geries, 'Christian-Muslim Dialog in the Holy Land', in *Cornerstone*, 64 (Winter 2012), p. 5.

Khoury, Fr Rafiq, 'Living together: the Experience of Muslim-Christian Relations in the Arab world in general and in Palestine in particular', in *Cornerstone*, 64 (Winter 2012), pp. 10-12.

Kim, Kirsteen, *The Holy Spirit in the World – A Global Conversation* (London: SPCK, 2007).

Lane, Dermot, *Stepping Stones to other Religions: a Christian Theology of Inter-religious Dialogue* (Dublin: Veritas Publications, 2011).

Lerner, Michael, *Embracing Israel-Palestine* (San Francisco: Tikkun Books, 2011).

MacRory, Joseph, 'St. Mark', in *The Catholic Encyclopedia*, vol. 9 (New York: Robert Appleton Company, 1910),

Mark the Deacon, *Life of Porphyry* (Oxford: Oxford Clarendon Press, 1913).

McDonnell, Kilian, *The Other Hand of God: The Holy Spirit as the Universal Touch and Goal* (Collegeville: Liturgical Press, 2003).

McIhagga, Kate, *The Green Heart of the Snowdrop* (Glasgow: Wild Goose Publications, 2004).

McIntyre, John, *Faith, Theology and Imagination* (Edinburgh, 1987).

A Moment of Truth: A word of faith, hope, and love from the heart of Palestinian suffering (Jerusalem: Kairos, 2009).

Murphy-O'Connor, Jerome, *Jesus and Paul: Parallel Lives* (Minnesota, Collegeville: Michael Glazier Liturgical Press, 2007).

Neuhaus, Fr David, 'Christian-Jewish Relations in the Contest of Israel-Palestine', in *Cornerstone*, 64 (Winter 2012), p. 6–8.

Priestland, Gerald, *Priestland's Progress: One Man's Search for Christianity Now* (London: Ariel Books, 1981).

Rahner, Karl, 'Frömmigkeit Früher und Heute', in *Schriften zur Theologie*, VII (Einsiedeln/Zurich/Koln: Verlaganstalt Benziger and Co., 1966), pp. 11-31.

Rayan, Samuel, *The Holy Spirit - Heart of the Christian Gospel* (Maryknoll: Orbis, 1978).

Ruether, Rosemary Radford, *Faith and Fratricide: the Theological Roots of Anti-Semitism* (New York: The Seabury Press, 1974).

Sherry, Patrick, *Spirit and Beauty: an Introduction to Theological Aesthetics* (London: SCM, 1992, reprinted 2002).

Soelle, Dorothee, 'Breaking the Ice of the Soul: Theology and Literature in Search of a New Language,' in Pinnock (ed.), *The Theology of Dorothee Soelle*, pp. 31-53.

Soelle, Dorothee, *The Silent Cry: Mysticism and Resistance*, Rumscheidt, Barbara and Martin (trans.) (Minneapolis: Fortress, 2001).

Soelle, Dorothee, 'Liberating our God-Talk: From Authoritarian Otherness to Mystical Inwardness', in King, Ursula (ed.), *Liberating Women: New Theological Directions* (Bristol: University of Bristol Press, 1991), pp. 40-52;

South, Colin, 'Accepting the Fact of Death, We are freed to live more fully', in Harrow, Leonard (ed.), *Living Stones Yearbook 2012* (London: Living Stones of the Holy Land Trust, 2012), pp. 120-142.

Taylor, John V., *The Go-Between God* (London: Collins, 1972).

Time for Action: A British Response to A Moment of Truth, *the Kairos Palestine Document* (August 2013), <http://www.kairosbritain.org.uk>.

Tutu, Desmond, *No Future without Forgiveness* (New York: Random House, 1999).

Weil, Simone, *Waiting on God: The Essence of Her Thought*, Crauford, Emma (trans.) (London: Collins Fount Paperbacks, 1977).

Williams, Rowan, *Silence and Honey Cakes: the Wisdom of the Desert* (Oxford: Lion Publishing, 2003).

Reports from NGOs, charities, etc.

Aid to the Church in Need, *Persecuted and Forgotten: Report on Christians Oppressed for their Faith* (London: ACN, October 2013).

Save the Children, *Untold Atrocities: the Story of Syria's Children* (London, 2012).

'Two million Syrians are refugees', UNHCR Press Release (3 September 2013), <http://www.unhcr.org/522484fc9.html>.

The Day After: supporting a Democratic Transition in Syria (Syria: The Day After, 2012), <http://thedayafter-sy.org>.

Lightning Source UK Ltd.
Milton Keynes UK
UKOW06f1255260315

248584UK00008B/123/P

9 781908 381200